CRYSTAL HEALING

CRYSTAL HEALING

THE COMPLETE MODERN GUIDE
for beginners + beyond

YULIA VAN DOREN
GOLDIROCKS

Photography by Angela Nunnink,
Erika Raxworthy, and Yulia Van Doren

Hardie Grant
QUADRILLE

Contents

Crystal Index

Note: If you are looking for a crystal not listed here, see Alternative Crystal Names (pages 36—37), and Crystals + Color (pages 38—39).

From my intuition,
to yours

Hello, magic maker.

Whether you're already a devoted member of the crystal-obsessed club (never far from at least a few beloved rocks), or are very newly crystal-curious (and wondering what all the fuss is about?) — welcome! I am so glad you have found your way here.

When I wrote my first crystal book in 2017, my vision was to create a space where **everyone** felt welcome and included. Although hard to believe now, just a few short years ago crystal healing was still quite 'underground.' Every book, website, and social media account I could find about the metaphysical side of crystals fell into two distinct niches: Hippie-Eclectic *(think: obscure esoteric concepts, rainbow tie-dye, and nag champa galore)*, or Witchy-Occult *(complex rituals, black cats, and allll the moody filters)*. And though I have a very special place in my heart for all things hippie and witchy, I had an unshakeable intuition that something very important was happening worldwide: there was a growing number of people who were newly exploring alternative healing modalities like crystals, but who would feel intimidated by overly hippie or witchy vibes. Out of place, like they didn't belong. Like crystal healing and magic weren't meant for someone like them.

I am a lifelong, devoted student of metaphysics and alternative healing modalities, and I knew from personal experience that nothing could be further from the truth. **Crystals hold magic for ALL — no tie-dye or black cats required** *(and, by the way, no green-juice-routine or yoga-perfected-abs required, either!).*

I've made it my mission to bring crystal healing into the mainstream. Because to me, mainstream, isn't a bad word; I can't imagine anything more wonderful than a world where things like mindfulness and holistic healing are regular, everyday activities — can you?

Everyone is welcome here. Exactly as you are.

HOW TO USE THIS BOOK

My intention with this book is to swing open the door to the rainbow world of crystals, hold your hand while you cross the threshold — and then get out of your way! Because your *own* intuition will be your biggest superpower when it comes to crystal healing. You get to make your own intuitive discoveries and cosmic connections, perfectly aligned to your unique energy and healing.

This book combines my previous crystal books into one comprehensive guide, completely updated, expanded, and upleveled. It is divided into two parts: first, we'll cover all the information and tools needed to jumpstart your crystalline adventures, plus tips and techniques for crystallizing just about every facet of your everyday life. And the heart of this book is **THE CRYSTALS**, my in-depth guide to over 150 crystals and minerals that I believe hold the most magic and healing for our current time.

If this book has found its way to you, crystals hold magic for you to discover and experience. Trust your intuition, trust the power of magic, and keep your heart and spirit always open to the gifts that crystals will — magically, mysteriously, and most certainly — bring into your life.

I am so grateful to be able to share this magic with you.

Yulia
(aka Goldirocks)

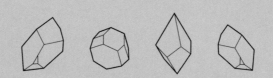

Crystals 101

Start here: An easy-to-understand overview of everything you need to know to get started with crystals.

You are made of stardust

"we are stardust,
billion year old carbon,
we are golden..."
Joni Mitchell, Woodstock

Everything within and surrounding you at this very moment was born from stardust. Created by ancient cosmic events of unimaginable power and immensity, stardust infuses our entire universe, and seeded life here on Planet Earth. And what is stardust? Stardust = minerals, minerals, and more minerals.

As Madonna (almost!) sang, we truly are *"living in a mineral world."* Beneath our feet lie unimaginable quantities and varieties of minerals within the earth. Above our heads sparkle the mineral clusters we call stars. Our buildings are crafted from minerals and crystals (steel = iron minerals, glass = melted crystals). Our cars, computers, and phones work only because they contain a multitude of minerals and crystals that literally power them. Crystal technology isn't just some woo-woo, new age concept; it is one of the essential building blocks of our modern technological age.

Modern technology already utilizes the scientifically proven powers of certain crystals, such as *piezoelectricity* (their ability to transform pressure into an electrical current), and *pyroelectricity* (their ability to generate an electric current when heated or cooled). However, there is a rapidly expanding community of people who are experiencing new powers contained within crystals and minerals — powers we believe modern science simply hasn't caught up with yet.

The mythology of crystals and minerals is as ancient and global as our human history. **It is your birthright.** You don't need special training or knowledge to begin experiencing the power of crystals, and you certainly don't need to spend loads of money on expensive pieces. All you need to get started is a sense of wonder and open-minded curiosity towards the one-of-a-kind, magnificent, magical creations that are crystals and minerals.

Let's get started.

Minerals and crystals and rocks, oh my...

Our beautiful planet contains over 5,000 identified minerals, with new varieties discovered each year; many crystal healers feel that new minerals surface as their specific energy is needed within the world. I like to be informal when talking about minerals / crystals / rocks / gemstones / stones and interchange terms, but let's take a moment to get clear on their unique differences:

MINERALS are generally formed from **only one chemical composition**; more than one and they turn into *rocks*. To qualify as a mineral, a substance must check these boxes: 1) It must form naturally; 2) It must be solid; 3) It must be formed primarily from inorganic material; 4) It must have an internal crystalline structure. Many minerals don't form crystals large enough to see with the human eye; *microcrystalline / masses* are terms used to describe these minerals. Examples of microcrystalline minerals: *Carnelian, Labradorite, Malachite*

CRYSTALS are minerals with a **visible crystallized form**. When a mineral crystallizes, its atoms are arranged in an orderly, repeating pattern, which results in the formation of a three-dimensional geometric shape. The astounding variety of crystals fits into just seven geometric categories, or *crystal systems*, making crystal identification easier than it might seem at first glance. Examples of crystals: *Clear Quartz, Fluorite, Pyrite*

ROCKS are generally formed from **grains of multiple minerals fused together** into a solid mass. And rocks may be formed from organic material, while true minerals cannot. Examples of rocks: *Jasper, Obsidian, Shungite*

GEMSTONES are minerals or rocks that are **hard** enough to be cut and polished for jewelry and decorative objects. Only about 200 mineral / rock varieties are able to be shaped into gemstones. *Precious gemstones* are a small group of highly valued gemstones, prized for their rarity, durability and beauty. *Semi-precious gemstones* are also valued for their beauty, but they are not as rare as precious gemstones, and therefore not as expensive. Examples of gemstones: *Diamond, Opal, Turquoise*

STONES is a non-technical term, commonly used in the mineral world to refer to small specimens whose rough edges have been mechanically polished away, i.e. **tumbled stones** or **polished stones**.

HOW CRYSTALS HEAL:

VIBRATION + COLOR + TALISMAN

Bringing sparkle and flash wherever they're placed, crystals top the list of nature's most stunning creations, and have a long history of being treasured for their physical beauty. However, their magic goes much deeper than just what meets the eye, and even when crystals are acquired purely for their good looks they can't help but infuse the spaces — and people — around them with their powerful combination of vibrational balancing, color healing, and talismanic magic.

VIBRATION As the otherworldly inventor, Nikola Tesla, put it, *"If you want to find the secrets of the universe, think in terms of energy, frequency, and vibration."* All of life dances with a magnetic pulse and vibration; scientists have learned that every atom in the universe is constantly in motion, and metaphysicians teach us that every object is surrounded by its own vibrating sphere of energy — an *aura*. Crystals are unique within nature as their atoms follow the most symmetrical pattern possible, creating what is called a *crystal lattice*. **It is their perfect atomic symmetry that makes crystals such powerful holders and transmitters of energy and vibration**. Because being a human is a much 'messier' atomic arrangement, our human atoms and auras are harmonized by interacting with the unique symmetry of crystals. And harmony = health.

COLOR The tradition of using color for health and wellbeing has been practiced since ancient times, and **the vibrant colors of crystals are one of the most potent aspects of their healing power**. Science has proven that we are profoundly affected by the colors that surround us, both physically and emotionally (don't you feel different in a bright-red versus pastel-blue room?). On a metaphysical level, our chakra system is activated by specific colors (*see page 52*). Crystals can change your mood and energy purely with their rainbow hues, and they provide one of the easiest ways to add pops of color to your physical spaces — they'll outlast any bouquet!

TALISMAN Born from the ancient Greek word *telein*, meaning 'to initiate into mysteries,' a talisman is traditionally defined as an object believed to hold magical abilities, lucky charms being the talismans us modern folk are usually most familiar with. When you make the choice to bring a crystal into your life for a specific intention — Rose Quartz to find love, or Citrine to gain confidence, for example — **your intention transforms the crystal into your personalized, magic-filled talisman**. That crystal is now your personal accountability buddy and cheerleader: it will tirelessly give both your consciousness and subconsciousness helpful nudges whenever you're near, reminding you of the energies you wish to hold, the person you wish to be, and the life you are ready to step into.

Q. How will crystals make me feel?
A. Crystals usually manifest their magic in what could be called 'subtle healing,' similar to many other holistic healing modalities. To better understand the concept of subtle healing, imagine the difference between drinking a glass of wine and taking a vitamin. After just a few sips of wine you feel unmistakably altered, but the effect is fleeting. In contrast, when you pop a vitamin you usually feel no different immediately, and may even begin to wonder whether taking vitamins is effective. Take those vitamins daily, however, and one day you suddenly realize, *"Wow, I feel so much better! That issue I've been having simply hasn't been bothering me… I haven't even thought about it lately!"* **Almost without you noticing, things have subtly — yet unmistakably — shifted within you**. Crystal healing often works via this form of subtle, long-term magic. That said, I've also experienced breathtakingly spontaneous and unexplainable moments of holistic healing. So my best advice is this: keep your mind and heart open to limitless possibilities, and you will be amazed by what manifests around and within you.

Q. What is 'holistic healing'?
A. Holistic healing focuses on treating the whole person — mind, body, and spirit — rather than only physical symptoms. It is based on the belief that all aspects of your life are interconnected, and that all areas need to be given attention, care, and love for optimal health.

Q. What is 'energy'?
A. Energy is that 'thing' which infuses, well, *everything*. It's been given many names over the years, from God to Spirit to Intuition to Magic. There's still plenty of mystery around energy and holistic healing — many things science hasn't been able to explain (yet) — but one thing is certain: energy is flowing around, through, and within you at this very moment.

A note about religion + crystals:
I've had some people new to crystals share with me their concern that crystal healing might in some way go against their religious beliefs. If you also have this worry, I wish to reassure you: **crystals are non-denominational holy tools**. Each and every crystal was created by whomever — or whatever — you believe created our universe. By treasuring their one-of-a-kind magnificence, you honor the Source of everything. By using crystals as healing tools, you allow the Spirit of healing to flow into our world with greater abundance — and I've yet to encounter a religion against that!

GET CRYSTALLIZED: crystal collecting

We are in the middle of a crystal heyday, with crystals sold
everywhere from huge chain stores to hipster coffee shops
(meaning it's never been easier to feed a crystal addiction
— you've been warned!).

GETTING STARTED

If you've spent any time exploring crystals,
you've probably already noticed a range
of differing — sometimes even conflicting
— metaphysical meanings assigned by
different sources to the same crystal.
Confused which description to trust?
Use that magical intuition of yours: if one
description resonates more than another,
follow that. Remember, crystals hold
multidimensional magic, meaning they
each have many metaphysical facets. **Your
intuition is how crystals will communicate
directly with you**. Very often, the first crystal
to catch your eye while browsing — or the
first you pick up — is the crystal that holds
the most magic for you right now. Don't
overthink it!

One way to intuitively grow your crystal
collection is to use the second half of this

book as an intuitive tool. Similar to pulling
an oracle card, this is a magical way to be
guided to the crystal most helpful for you.
Take a few calming breaths, close your eyes,
and intuitively open to a crystal profile. I'm
still regularly amazed by how this process
leads people to exactly the magic they need.

CRYSTAL SHOPPING

IN-PERSON Besides specialty mineral
stores, metaphysical (new age) shops are
generally the best option for in-person
crystal shopping. Mineral shows can also
be great for buying crystals IRL, filled with
friendly rockhounds and deals; google your
location + 'mineral show' to see if your
area has one. **If you need help deciding
whether to purchase a specific crystal,
close your eyes and hold it to your heart
or belly. After a few breaths, you should
get a clear intuitive sense whether the**

crystal is meant to come home with you right now. Note: It's common to begin to feel energetically overwhelmed while crystal shopping, especially at larger mineral shows. There's a lot of energy zooming around! If you start to feel light-headed or spacey, rub your palms together vigorously, and imagine roots coming out of your feet, anchoring you into the ground. You can also hold a grounding crystal until you feel better (Black Tourmaline or Hematite are great choices).

ONLINE One blessing of our modern age is that you're no longer limited to just what your local crystal shop has in stock (and that's if you're lucky enough to live near one!). Online crystal shopping is a vast world of sparkling options — from Etsy and eBay, to social media and beautiful boutiques — and I've purchased many of my favorite crystals online. A few tips for remorse-free online shopping: understand whether you'll receive the exact crystal photographed, double-check the crystal's size (centimeters and inches are very different!), and be cautious of too-good-to-be-true prices. Above all, make sure you purchase crystals from a business whose vibration and ethos you resonate with, as your crystal will have spent time in that vibrational environment.

YOU DON'T NEED TO SPEND $$
Some of my most treasured crystals are the most unassuming to look at. Dinged and scratched, chipped and cloudy, they aren't crystals that win beauty prizes, and they weren't pricey, but they just felt *right* when I saw them. **Powerful magic is often contained within humble exteriors**. Again, always trust your intuition when choosing your crystals, even if your eyes don't agree at first.

LOCAL STONES
Don't overlook the humble stones that live beneath your feet. They contain specific earth energies of the place in which you live, and are invaluable for **grounding yourself in current time and place** (vital for mental peace and stability). Stones from places meaningful to you — your birthplace, family home, beloved vacation spot, etc — are also valuable holders of energies important to your personal story, and I highly recommend including them in your collection.

CRYSTAL
CARE

Cleansing and charging your crystals' energy — especially when you first bring them home — is an important part of being a crystal owner. Have fun experimenting with the methods and rituals on the following pages, and discovering which most resonate with you and your crystals.

PROGRAM

Programming a crystal establishes a specific intention for your crystal to hold, usually for an energy or result you wish to manifest. While doing so can be very powerful, programming is not always necessary. It's important to remember that crystals hold an innate intelligence that works on levels beyond our human understanding; crystal consciousness is most transformative when we allow it to work *with* us, not *for* us. Crystals are powerful consciousness-raising helpers; let's make sure to not limit their magic by overly controlling them! So only program a crystal if your intuition clearly guides you to do so, and if it doesn't, trust that the crystal is already aligned with your highest healing and transformation. *See page 29 to learn how to program.*

MAINTENANCE

Monthly moonbaths give crystals a powerful recharge, and are often all they need to remain fully charged and activated. Also regularly check that your crystals aren't covered in a fine layer of dust, which dulls both their physical beauty and metaphysical magic. Clean them with a quick water rinse, power breath, or small brush (makeup brushes work well).

ENERGY IS ENERGY IS ENERGY...

Although it makes me a bit of a rebel in the crystal world, I don't align with the belief that crystals easily pick up 'bad' or 'negative' energy, and that you shouldn't let others touch your crystals for fear they might get contaminated by your friends' less-than-perfect vibes. **Energy is simply energy, neither good nor bad**. It's human nature to want to assign a characteristic to energy, but in truth, what's considered good by someone might be considered bad by another; it's personal preference. To worry that your crystals need constant cleansing and 'protection' not only keeps you too focused on the negative — not where you want your attention to live — it disregards the innate power and intelligence within crystals themselves. Have faith that your crystals can keep themselves clear and high-vibrational! That said, please follow your intuition with this; you can set any boundaries you wish around your crystals.

BREATH + INTENTION

Breath combined with intention is the simplest and quickest cleansing option.

RITUAL Holding your crystal in front of you, inhale through your nose. Envision a golden light filling your lungs. Exhale that light through your mouth with quick, gently forceful breaths, like you're blowing out candles on a birthday cake. Repeat several times, until you intuitively sense that all energy cobwebs have been blown away, and your crystal is visually cleared of any dust or dirt.

SUNLIGHT

Sunlight melts away stale energies, and is an extremely activating force.

RITUAL While not all crystals are meant to be sun-worshippers, sunshine is a very powerful cleanser and most crystals benefit from at least a short sunbath when you first bring them home. Place your crystal in a sunlit area, such as a windowsill, for at least a few hours. I personally love displaying my crystals in sunny spots, as they sparkle so beautifully, but if you choose to keep a crystal in a bright area long-term, you must be at peace with the fact that it may fade over time. Note: if prolonged sun exposure is of extra concern, I've noted it in the crystal's profile.

MOONLIGHT

Moonlight is supercharging, and safe for all crystals.

RITUAL There is mysterious magic in moonlight, and crystals thrive on regular moonbaths. Moonlight is safe for every crystal, unlike sunlight. Lay your crystals overnight in a place where moonlight will touch them (windowsills and tables near a window work well). As many metallic minerals can rust in overnight dew, use caution with outdoor charging. The light of a full or new moon is extra magical, and moonbaths under these supercharged moons will keep your crystals very happy and healthy.

SMOKE

The cleansing smoke from burning herbs moves and purifies energy.

RITUAL Light your favorite source of herbal smoke, and hold your crystal in the stream of smoke for several moments. For an extra boost of magic, rotate the smoke around your crystal seven times, in a clockwise motion. There are many popular varieties of herbal smoke. Sage and palo santo have powerful cleansing energies, however as both are endangered resources it's important to source them sustainably. A great alternative is local dried herbs (cedar, lavender, and rose are personal favorites). Incense sticks are also a convenient option.

♪ SOUND
Music's vibrational waves harmonize everything they touch.

RITUAL Chant, ring, drum, strum! Crystals love being around music, and live music especially brings them to life, and infuses them with a special vibrance. So strum that guitar, chant your mantra, and ring bells and singing bowls near your crystals whenever possible. Don't be shy; crystals are the most non-judgemental audience one could ask for!

◌ WATER
Water is nature's most potent cleanser and purifier.

RITUAL Rinse your crystal gently under a running tap, or submerge briefly in a bowl of water. If you live near a freshwater source, it can be extra-magical to use local water; fill a bottle to bring home, or take your crystals to the water source to give them the special gift of being cleansed in nature (saltwater can be abrasive, so steer clear of ocean and sea water). Important: there are quite a few minerals that rust or weaken from water exposure, so do your research first; if in any doubt, use a different cleansing method. To make it easy for you, I've listed in each crystal's profile lists whether water exposure is safe.

⬒ EARTH
'Earthing' in soil grounds and recharges.

RITUAL Place your crystal on or under the soil of a houseplant, or bury under a few inches of soil outside if you have that option — just don't forget to clearly mark where you left them, many crystals have returned to the earth this way! Leave for at least one night, as long as intuitively feels right. Earthing is especially good for crystals with grounding properties, and those that have traveled through airport scanners with you. Note: earthing should not be done with water-sensitive minerals, as the moisture in soil can damage them.

◇ SALT
Salt is purifying, but should be used with caution as can cause damage.

RITUAL Although popular, I don't recommend using salt as a general cleansing method, as it can damage and weaken crystals. However, if you use crystals for healing treatments on other people (in a spa or massage studio, for instance), salt can be a good option for keeping your 'worker' crystals fresh. Fill a bowl or tray with Himalayan salt (coarse is best, as smaller granules can cause damage by getting into clusters) and place your crystals on the salt for at least 10 minutes between sessions.

A few favorite smoke-cleansing options:
palo santo, white sage, and bundles of cedar and roses.

OPPOSITE
Himalayan Samadhi Quartz charging on a sunny windowsill.

NEW CRYSTAL CARE
QUICK GUIDE

The following is my go-to ritual when I bring new crystals home.
Quick, easy, and very effective!

1) CLEANSE + CHARGE

Hold your crystal in your non-dominant hand, close your eyes, and take three slow, calm breaths to ground yourself. If your crystal has visible dust, clear it away with a few power breaths. Imagine a beam of shimmering golden light rising from the core of the earth, flowing through your body, and radiating out through the crystal you hold.

Say aloud: *"Now release all energies that are not of this time and place. Keep only energies that serve the highest good. You are cleansed and cleared with love and light."*

Place the crystal in either sunlight or moonlight to charge for at least four hours.

2) CONNECT

To connect your energy with your new crystal, hold it to your corresponding chakra point (*see page 52 for a chakra chart*), and take three slow, deep breaths. Imagine the crystal glowing from the inside, infusing your entire body and aura with its color. If you wish, say its affirmation aloud. Repeat the process with each chakra point (some crystals resonate with just one chakra, many resonate with several).

3) PROGRAM

If you wish to program your crystal for a specific purpose, hold your crystal with both hands, and imagine it surrounded by a shimmering golden light. Say aloud the intention you wish the crystal to hold for you: *"I program this crystal for (e.g. healing my heart / protecting me while I travel / strengthening my willpower to make healthy choices). For the highest good of all, in love and in light."*

Remember: specific crystal programming isn't always necessary, so if you don't feel led to program your crystal, trust that its magic is already aligned to your specific needs and healing.

CRYSTAL SHAPES

The shape of a crystal affects how its magic flows into the world. From nature-made shapes such as clusters and geodes, to human-made shapes such as palm stones and pyramids, each form holds its own unique power, and can help you access different aspects of crystalline healing and magic. Here's your quick guide to the classics.

1) NATURAL POINT *(a naturally formed faceted point)* Like a magic wand, crystal points focus and move energy. Change the direction of the point to draw energy towards you, or direct energy away from you. Perfect for focusing on specific intentions and desires, and for directing healing energy to a specific spot on the body.

2) CLUSTER *(a group of natural points)* Clusters radiate energy in all directions (like a crystal disco ball!), infusing all surrounding spaces and auras.

3) GEODE *(a hollow, crystal-lined rock)* Geodes remind us that true magic lives *within*, beyond the surface. True healing requires a deep dive. Go deeper.

4) SPHERE *(ball)* Round crystals emit energy in all directions in a balanced, equalized flow. Holding or gazing at a sphere can be calming, balancing, and grounding.

5) CUBE *(square / rectangular)* Both natural and shaped cubic crystals are highly grounding and stabilizing. Great for thinking outside the box, and seeing problems with fresh eyes.

6) PALM STONE *(polished + flat)* Palm stones are popular for on-body crystal healing, as their shape makes them easy to place on the body. Very grounding and soothing to hold.

7) TUMBLED STONE *(polished + rounded)* Affordable and easily transportable, these are the workhorses of crystal healing. Easy to stash in a multitude of spots (like your pocket / bag / wallet / bra / car / bath / bed) to keep crystal magic close at all times.

8) PYRAMID *(four equal triangular sides)* An ancient sacred shape, pyramids connect heaven and earth. They gather and channel energy through their point, and are potent manifestation tools.

9) DOUBLE-TERMINATED *(a crystal with points on both ends)* Double-terminated crystals are very powerful, as they can simultaneously transmit and amplify energy in both directions. The best crystals for moving stuck energy.

10) GENERATOR *(a crystal with six facets that join together in one point)* Generators amplify energy. Great centerpieces for grids to manifest intentions. Polished generators are more common than natural.

11) PHANTOM *(a quartz crystal with an internal 'shadow' point)* Phantoms help keep things in perspective. They remind you to honor the wisdom and lessons contained in your history, both from this lifetime and past lives.

12) SOULMATE *(two crystals joined together along one side)* Soulmates are magical for working through relationship issues, as well as for manifesting soulmates (both romantic and platonic).

13) SELF-HEALED *(a quartz crystal with small bumps/scales on one end)* These are crystals that started to regrow after breaking. Self-healed crystals remind you that you are resilient, and help heal pain, trauma and heartbreak.

14) ELESTIAL *(a quartz crystal with multiple random terminations)* Elestials are unusual crystals that can help you work through past-life experiences, as well as remove blockages around change.

15) RECORD-KEEPER *(a crystal with triangular markings)* Ancient spiritual wisdom. Place on your 3rd eye *(between your eyebrows)* to begin to download esoteric knowledge, and upgrade your energy.

16) ABUNDANCE *(one long point surrounded by tiny points)* Abundance clusters = manifest abundance!

17) RAW *(unaltered)* Raw crystals hum with organic magic. They are reminders that nature does not make mistakes, and that everything is uniquely beautiful in its natural form — like, for example, YOU.

POLISHED VS RAW

Perhaps similar to the idea that getting your nutrients from real food is more potent than a vitamin, many crystal lovers find something inherently organic and powerful about a crystal left in its 'raw' form, as created by Mother Earth. There are, however, many minerals that reveal hidden glamour only once polished: Agate and Rainbow Fluorite's colorful layers are much more visible when polished, as is the flash within Labradorite and Moonstone, as examples. Polished crystals can also be easier to place on the body for on-body healing, and they're very handy for carrying around in all those spots we love to tuck our rocks (bags, pockets, bras, etc). Just be aware that polishing a crystal can sometimes unnaturally 'freeze' its energy flow, so if a polished crystal doesn't feel alive to you, definitely try to get your hands on a raw specimen for comparison — the energetic difference can be quite amazing! *(Pictured: polished, half-polished, and raw Sunstone crystals.)*

A note about mining:

*Mining is a complicated subject with imperfect truths but, as mindful crystal collectors, it's important to address. Look around yourself right now: almost everything surrounding you exists because of mined minerals, from the paper or screen you're reading this on, to the roof you're sitting under, to the glass jar your latest organic purchase came in. It's one of the complex truths of our modern age: more people live on this planet than ever before, enjoying a quality of life better than previous generations could have ever imagined, and what makes it all possible? Mining. Iron-based minerals such as Hematite are melted for steel, lithium-filled minerals like Lepidolite become batteries and pharmaceuticals, our TV and computer screens wouldn't work without Celestite, Aragonite becomes fertilizer, etc etc etc... the list is practically endless. Many of the minerals mined today formed before our first ancestors walked this earth, are of extremely limited quantity, and I passionately believe they deserve better than being destroyed to make something that will ultimately end up in a trash landfill. **If we didn't place value on keeping minerals in their whole form, they would almost certainly be destroyed for industrial use.** I'm not trying to avoid the obvious: yes, the mining industry as a whole needs much reform and oversight. We all need to be asking questions and pushing for change, especially on the industrial level, and — most crucially! — changing our own lifestyles so that less mining is needed overall. And alongside that, please also take the best care of each of your crystals. Consider this remarkable truth: with proper care, a crystal lover generations from now could treasure the very same crystals you do. We are only their caretakers for the present moment.*

ALTERNATIVE CRYSTAL NAMES

As crystal healing continues to grow in popularity, many varieties are given new names by crystal dealers and healers. It can get quite confusing, especially as a mineral's 'new' name sometimes becomes better-known than its original. To help, here's a list of common alternative names you're likely to come across, as well as popular human-made (aka artificial) varieties.

African Jade — see *Garnet (Grossular)*

Agnitite — see *Hematite Quartz*

Alexandrite — see *Chrysoberyl*

Amazon Jade — see *Amazonite*

Ammolite — see *Ammonite*

Andara Crystal — glass

Anhydrite — see *Angelite*

Anyolite — see *Ruby Zoisite*

Apache Tears — see *Obsidian*

Aquaprase — see *Chrysoprase*

Atlantisite/Atlantasite — see *Serpentine*

Atlantis Stone — see *Larimar*

Aventurine Glass — glass

Bismuth — almost always lab-grown

Blueberry Quartz — glass

Blue John — see *Fluorite*

Bolivianite — see *Ametrine* or *Serpentine*

Bornite — see *Peacock Ore*

Cat's Eye — see *Chrysoberyl*

Cactus Quartz — see *Spirit Quartz*

Calligraphy Stone — see *Jasper*

Cave Calcite — see *Aragonite*

Celestine — see *Celestite*

Chalcopyrite — see *Peacock Ore*

Cherry Quartz — glass

Chlorite Quartz — see *Lodolite*

Cinnamon Stone — see *Garnet (Hessonite)*

Copal — see *Amber*

Crackle Quartz — artificially cracked

Cubic Zirconia (CZ) — lab-grown

Diamond Quartz — see *Herkimer Diamond*

Dolphin Stone — see *Larimar*

Dragon's Blood — see *Jasper (Dragon's Blood)*

Fairy Quartz — see *Spirit Quartz*

Fire + Ice Quartz — artificially cracked

Fire Quartz — see *Hematite Quartz*

Fool's Gold — see *Pyrite*

Garden Quartz — see *Lodolite*

Garnierite — see *Serpentine*

Gem Silica — see *Chalcedony / Chrysocolla*

Goboboseb — see *Brandberg Amethyst*

Goldstone — glass

Harlequin Quartz — see *Hematite Quartz*

Hawk's Eye — see *Tiger's Eye*

Healerite — see *Serpentine*

Helenite — glass, also called Gaia Stone

Heliotrope — see *Bloodstone*

Heulandite — see *Stilbite*

Hiddenite — see *Kunzite*

Iceland Spar — see *Optical Calcite*

Inclusion Quartz — see *Lodolite*

Infinite Stone — see *Serpentine*

Jadeite — see *Jade*

K2 — see *Jasper (K2)*

Larvikite — see *Labradorite*

Lavulite / Luvulite — see *Sugilite*

Lemon Quartz — see *Citrine*

Lepidocrocite — see *Hematite Quartz*

Lizardite — see *Serpentine*

Magnesite — see *Howlite*

Merlinite — see *Common Opal (Dendritic)*

Moissanite — lab-grown

Mugglestone — see *Tiger's Eye*

Muscovite — see *Fuchsite*

Nephrite — see *Jade*

New Jade — see *Serpentine*

Olivine — see *Peridot*

Opalite — glass

Pink Amethyst — see *Hematite Quartz*

Prase — see *Chrysoprase*

Prasiolite — heat-treated Amethyst

Rock Crystal — see *Clear Quartz*

Sard — see *Carnelian*

Satin Spar — see *Selenite*

Schorl — see *Black Tourmaline*

Shaman Quartz — see *Lodolite*

Spectrolite — see *Labradorite*

Strawberry Quartz — often glass; see *Hematite Quartz*

Tiger Iron — see *Tiger's Eye*

Transvaal Jade — see *Garnet (Grossular)*

Turquenite — see *Howlite*

Verdite — see *Fuchsite*

White Buffalo Stone — see *Howlite*

Zebra Stone — see *Jasper (Zebra)*

CRYSTALS + COLOR

If you wish to connect with a crystal that isn't given its own profile in this book, this chart is here to help. **The colors of crystals are one of the best ways to understand and connect with their healing magic.** Simply match the primary color of your crystal with this chart to discover its healing properties, the chakra(s) it resonates with, and affirmations for activating a connection between you and your crystal.

BLACK / GRAY (Root)
Protection. Grounding. Stabilizing. Strength. Detox. Shadow work. Energy shield. Release grief.

"I am safe + protected"

BROWN (Root, Sacral)
Stabilizing. Grounding. Balance. Slow-and-steady growth. Adaptability. Nature + natural cycles.

"I am nourished + grounded"

RED (Root, Sacral)
Action. Passion. Energy. Assertiveness. Stand-up-for-yourself. Courage. Strength. Grounding. Physical health. Fertility. Sexuality. Release pain, trauma, grief.

"I am supported"
"I am strong"

ORANGE (Sacral, Solar Plexus)
Manifestation. Creative fire. Confidence. Abundance. Willpower. Energy. Health. Fertility. Sexuality. Release sexual trauma.

"I am a creative powerhouse"
"I manifest with abundance + ease"

YELLOW / GOLD (Solar Plexus)

Confidence. Purpose. Stand-in-the-spotlight. Entrepreneurism. Ambition. Focus. Creativity. Abundance. Manifestation. Happiness.

"I trust my gut"
"I sparkle + shine"

PINK (Heart)

Love. Compassion. Heart-healing. Kindness. Comfort. Friendship. Forgiveness. Self-acceptance. Divine Feminine. Fertility.

"I am love"

GREEN (Heart)

Heart-healing. Natural health. Wellness. Luck. Abundance. Prosperity. Fairyworld magic. Connection to Mother Earth. Growth. Fertility.

"I am abundant"
"I am healthy"

BLUE (Throat, 3rd Eye)

Communication. Speak your truth. Connection to angels + intuition. Patience. Serenity. Cooling. Calming. Water + air magic.

"I trust my intuition"
"I flow my truth into the world"

PURPLE (Crown)

Connection to Higher Self. Spiritual growth. Leadership. Psychic intuition. Individuality. Dance-to-your-own-drum. Dreamtime messages. Insomnia remedy. Release addictions + anxieties.

"I am divinely guided"
"I am a Lightworker"

CLEAR / WHITE / SILVER
(3rd Eye, Crown)

Energy cleansing + clearing. Clarity. New beginnings. Protection. Angelic realm. Moon magic. Intuition. Manifestation. Balancing. Neutralizing. Transformation.

"I am a clear channel"
"All good things flow to me + through me"

RAINBOW (All)

Joy. Play. Exploration. Creativity. Self-expression. Confidence. Fun. Abundance.

"I am a child of the universe"

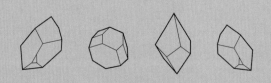

Everyday Magic

Now that you've learned the basics of what crystals are, and how they heal, it's time for the fun part — adding crystals to your daily life!

First stop: crystallizing your home, workspace, and body.

CRYSTALS + HOME

One of the best (and easiest!) ways to begin crystallizing your life is with intentionally placed crystals in your home. They will weave an energetic grid to support you and your loved ones 24 hours a day, and keep your home's energy fresh and sparkling.

Your home is so much more than just a very large box of your possessions. Whether you're living in your dream house or a temporary apartment, each room nourishes and supports you in specific ways, and decorating with crystals can transform your home into a magic-filled sanctuary. If you're unsure how to start, simply place a crystal where you might put a candle or houseplant, being mindful that some crystals fade in direct sunlight. Here are my favorites for crystallizing each room *(to choose between the crystals in each list, simply follow what intuitively speaks to you)*.

**ENTRANCE + HALLWAYS
(for protection + energy cleansing)**

Agate, Amethyst, Apophyllite, Citrine, Clear Quartz, Pyrite, Rose Quartz, Selenite, Smoky Quartz, Tourmaline (Black)
tip: keep a piece of Selenite by your front door to cleanse your energy when you return home.

**LIVING + DINING ROOMS
(for loving communication + relaxation)**

Amethyst, Apophyllite, Calcite (all), Celestite, Clear Quartz, Desert Rose, Himalayan Samadhi Quartz, Jasper (all), Kyanite, Lemurian Quartz, Rose Quartz, Spirit Quartz, Stilbite
tip: these crystals kept in busy living spaces do double duty as sparkling decor and powerful space-clearers.

KITCHEN
(for healthy choices + willpower)

Amethyst, Amber, Apatite, Bloodstone, Calcite, Carnelian, Citrine, Clear Quartz, Emerald, Epidote, Fluorite, Jasper, Pyrite, Selenite, Shungite, Smoky Quartz, Sunstone
tip: put crystals in your fridge and cupboards to infuse food with extra-healthy vibes.

BEDROOM
(for calm sleep + wise dreams)

Agate (Blue Lace), Angelite, Amethyst, Brandberg Amethyst, Calcite (Blue), Celestite, Chalcedony, Herkimer Diamond, Kambaba Jasper, Moonstone, Labradorite, Lemurian Quartz, Lepidolite, Lithium Quartz, Lodolite, Rose Quartz, Scolecite, Tourmaline (Black), Vera Cruz Amethyst
tip: for healing and guidance while you sleep, place crystals on your nightstand, or tuck them under your pillow, mattress, or bed frame.

BATHROOM
(for self-care + health)

Amethyst, Aquamarine, Citrine, Emerald, Jasper, Larimar, Morganite, Rose Quartz, Smoky Quartz, Unakite
tip: add any of these crystals to your bathwater for a full-body infusion.

CHILDREN'S ROOM
(for calm + angelic protection)

Agate (Blue Lace), Amethyst, Angelite, Calcite (Mangano), Celestite, Chalcedony, Herkimer Diamond, Lepidolite, Moonstone, Rose Quartz
tip: place any of these crystals near the crib or bed to encourage calm sleep. Be sure to keep crystals away from little mouths!

CRYSTALS + WORK

Like cosmic life coaches, crystals will cheer you on, inspire you to think bigger, and help you stay on track with your shiniest goals. Any combo of these crystals will uplevel your workday.

focus + productivity
Apophyllite, Calcite (Optical), Citrine, Desert Rose, Fluorite, Galena, Hematite, Obsidian, Pyrite, Selenite, Sunstone, Vanadinite

communication
Amazonite, Aquamarine, Celestite, Chrysocolla, Kyanite, Rose Quartz, Sodalite, Spirit Quartz

creativity + inspiration
Amethyst (all), Ametrine, Celestite, Clear Quartz, Golden Healer Quartz, Herkimer Diamond, Jasper (Mookaite / Picasso), Lapis Lazuli, Lemurian Quartz, Lodolite, Opal, Peacock Ore, Sapphire

abundance
Aventurine, Chrysoprase, Citrine, Emerald, Jade, Pyrite, Ruby, Rutilated Quartz

CRYSTALS + ZEN

Create a grounded healing vibration in your therapeutic spaces, both personal and professional: meditation room, yoga studio, spa, treatment room, etc. Keep the energies clear and flowing, and nurture your clients (and yourself) with the support of crystals for energy purification, grounding, wellness, and rejuvenation. These are my favorite crystals for healing spaces:

Amethyst (all), Apophyllite, Calcite (all), Celestite, Citrine, Clear Quartz, Desert Rose, Fluorite, Golden Healer Quartz, Herkimer Diamond, Himalayan Samadhi Quartz, Lemurian Quartz, Pyrite, Rose Quartz, Selenite, Smoky Quartz, Spirit Quartz, Stilbite, Tourmaline (Black)

tip: size often does matter when it comes to crystals for dedicated healing spaces, as they have to process a lot of energy. In general, the bigger, the better. Be sure to regularly cleanse these crystals.

CRYSTALS ON-THE-GO

Tumbled stones are perfect for keeping crystal magic flowing while you're out and about, and most crystal lovers always have a few rattling around their bags, wallets, pockets, and cars. You can tuck small crystals everywhere from bra cups to sock cuffs; follow your intuition on what will provide the best support for your upcoming day.

CRYSTALS + WELLNESS

SLEEP

Absorbing crystal energy while sleeping is extra potent. In addition to placing crystals on your nightstand, you can tuck small crystals into your pillowcase, between mattress and box spring, or place them under your bed for focused healing. Try putting an Amethyst under your head, a Rose Quartz under your heart, and a Black Tourmaline by your feet to experience one of my favorite nighttime layouts. Sleeping near a new crystal can be a magical way to connect with its energy; keep a journal close to record dreamtime insights. And pay attention to whether some crystals feel too 'activating' for your bedroom — I personally have a hard time sleeping near Tiger's Eye and Moldavite, for example.

BATHE

Add crystals to your bath to transform it into an extra-blissful self-care ritual. If you haven't experienced a crystallized bath, you have something special to look forward to! Tumbled stones are generally best for baths. Make sure not to use crystals that can dissolve or rust, or those containing lead or mercury (each crystal's profile lists whether water exposure is safe). See pages 233 and 260 for two of my favorite crystal bath rituals.

YOGA

Crystallize your asanas. If you practice at home, experiment with surrounding your yoga mat with different crystal combinations, and placing a crystal on your heart during *Savasana* (the final resting pose). For group classes, I often bring a small Rose Quartz and Carnelian to infuse my practice with compassionate self-care and willpower — I tuck them into my sports bra, or place at the edge of my mat.

ELIXIR

Drink your crystals! Giving new meaning to 'on the rocks,' drinkable crystal elixirs can be taken internally for powerful healing from the inside out. To make a crystal elixir, put one or more tumbled stones into a jar or pitcher, fill with water (filtered or spring water is best), and place in sunlight or moonlight for at least 12 hours to infuse and charge the water. Remove the crystals, and drink up for a lovely internal boost of crystal healing. Infused water does not expire; if you wish, keep several blends handy and drink as needed. *(Note: it is vitally important to use non-toxic stones for elixirs, so please do your research before experimenting.)*

Recipes:

Wellness
Carnelian + Rose Quartz
+ Amethyst

Self-Love
Rose Quartz + Clear Quartz

Detox
Shungite + Amethyst

Anxiety Relief
Amethyst + Smoky Quartz

WEAR

Adorning ourselves with gemstones is likely the oldest form of crystal healing. Humans throughout history have worn crystals for ceremony and ritual. Our ancestors were wise: wearing jewelry is not only beautiful, it is the ultimate way to envelop yourself in a crystal's energy, and keep its magic close as you live your daily life. Don't forget to cleanse and charge your jewelry every so often; moonlight, smoke, and sound are the safest methods. For an extra-magical recharge, on full moon nights leave your jewels in a moonlit spot overnight.

Birthstones are gemstones aligned with specific calendar months and zodiac signs, to help balance, enhance, and support innate energies. Turn the page to learn about this classic and beloved system for wearing crystals.

CRYSTALS + BIRTHSTONES

Our physical bodies are quite literally built from stardust (minerals!), so doesn't it make sense that we could be influenced by the movements of stars and planets? Crystals have been paired with astrology by diverse cultures for thousands of years. The modern birthstone chart is based on a variety of sources, including gemstones mentioned in the Hebrew bible, sacred Indian Vedic texts, ancient Greek treatises, and modern gemstone discoveries, and is a great place to start if you wish to connect with crystals specific to your birthdate.

MODERN BIRTHSTONES

JANUARY
Garnet

FEBRUARY
Amethyst

MARCH
Aquamarine / Bloodstone

APRIL
Diamond

MAY
Emerald

JUNE
Pearl / Moonstone / Alexandrite

JULY
Ruby

AUGUST
Peridot / Spinel

SEPTEMBER
Sapphire

OCTOBER
Opal / Tourmaline

NOVEMBER
Golden Topaz / Citrine

DECEMBER
Blue Topaz / Blue Zircon / Tanzanite / Turquoise

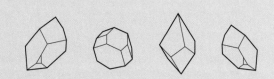

Crystals + Rituals

Now let's take your crystallizing to the next level: chakra healing, moon manifesting, and more...

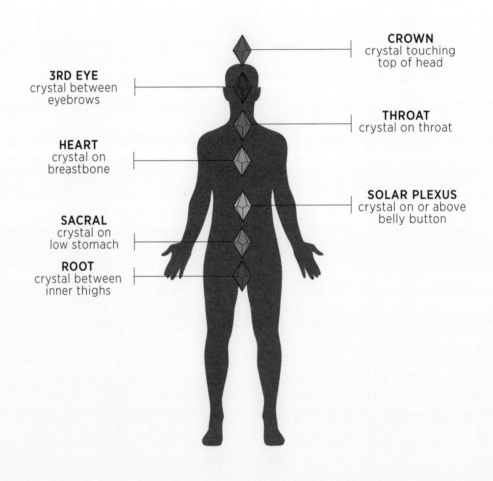

CROWN
crystal touching
top of head

3RD EYE
crystal between
eyebrows

THROAT
crystal on throat

HEART
crystal on
breastbone

SOLAR PLEXUS
crystal on or above
belly button

SACRAL
crystal on
low stomach

ROOT
crystal between
inner thighs

CRYSTALS + CHAKRAS:

YOU ARE A RAINBOW

chakra = *from ancient Sanskrit, meaning 'wheel'*

Placing crystals directly on specific points of the body activates powerful healing and recharging. Our bodies are powered by a rainbow-colored energy system known as chakras. First written about thousands of years ago by holy monks in ancient India, chakras are energy vortexes that vibrate within and around your body at specific points. We use our chakras constantly to both draw in and expend energy, and a well-working chakra system is absolutely vital to how healthy you feel — both physically and emotionally — and how vibrantly you are able to function in your day-to-day life. And if the charging port on your phone looks anything like mine, you won't have a hard time envisioning how necessary it is to regularly clear and recharge your chakras (aka your body's charging ports) from the gunk of daily life. Yoga, meditation, and time in nature are wonderful ways to keep your chakra system healthy, and crystals are potent, easy-to-use tools to add to your chakra health kit (I like to call them chakra vitamins!).

You have seven main chakras, each associated with a specific color and energy focus. They flow in rainbow order from the bottom of your spine to the top of your head. The chakra vortexes along the front of your body move your energy *out* into the world, and the equally important (often overlooked) chakra vortexes along the back of your body *receive* energy and input from your spiritual support staff — a direct hotline to your personal angels and guides. Crystal chakra healing can manifest in a myriad of ways. You might feel electric tingles, a deep sense of peace, spontaneously break out in tears or laughter, or you may even feel nothing at all. The reaction you have will always be the 'right' reaction; trust the process, trust your intuition, trust your crystals.

This chart shows where on your body each chakra is located, and its corresponding color. Experiment with the following chakra rituals to get started using crystals for on-body healing, and don't forget that there are limitless ways to heal with crystals. Have fun letting your intuition go ROYGBIV-wild!

CRYSTAL CHAKRA HEALING

Find a quiet moment and comfortable place to lie down. Kick off your shoes and turn your phone to silent. If you wish, stream calming background music, although silence is equally powerful. Drink plenty of water before and after.

SINGLE CHAKRA RECHARGE

MAGIC

This one-crystal ritual is great for a quick recharge, applying focused healing to a specific area, and for getting to know a new crystal's energy. You can set an alarm (I recommend 5 or 11 minutes), or simply finish when your intuition guides you.

RITUAL

Gently roll your crystal between your palms several times to activate it. Place it on your body in the area of the chakra you wish to charge, and begin breathing long, calm breaths. Imagine the crystal beginning to flow its color into your body. The color expands with every breath, until your entire body and aura are infused with glowing color. *You are in a shimmering, healing bubble.* Stay here, healing and recharging, until your alarm rings, or you intuitively feel finished.

Take one final deep inhale and exhale, and remove the crystal from your body while saying *"Thank You"* out loud — your gratitude lets the crystal know you are done charging, and unplugs its energy from your chakra.

COMPLETE CHAKRA RECHARGE

MAGIC
Gift a healing boost to your entire chakra system. This is powerful self-care — treat yourself as often as you wish. This ritual is also a healing gift to share with your loved ones, big and small. You can set an alarm (I recommend at least 11 minutes), or simply finish when your intuition guides you.

CRYSTALS NEEDED
• 7 crystals, one for each chakra
• 2 black or gray grounding crystals
• 2 Rose Quartz

RITUAL
Place the grounding crystals so they touch the sole of each foot. Place the seven crystals on your body, in order from the root chakra up. Hold a Rose Quartz in each hand to create a healing cocoon, and close your eyes. Begin breathing long, calm breaths. Notice the comforting weight of each crystal on your body, taking the time to really feel each one. Let your body feel deliciously weighted and grounded. Now, envision the crystals beginning to glow. Their shimmering color orbs expand with each of your breaths, larger and larger, until they merge into a giant rainbow bubble that completely surrounds you. Breathe this rainbow in with every breath; imagine the colors rushing through your veins, purifying and energizing every cell in your body. With every exhale, imagine color shimmering out of you in a beautiful rainbow cloud. *You are a rainbow.* Stay here, healing and recharging, until your alarm rings, or you intuitively feel finished.

When ready, remove the crystals from your body in the opposite order from which you placed them, saying *"Thank You"* out loud while removing each crystal — your gratitude tells the crystals you are done charging, and unplugs their energy from your chakra system. Please be sure to drink plenty of alkalizing water in the hours following this rainbow recharge!

CRYSTALS + THE MOON:

A MATCH MADE IN HEAVEN

Crystals + moon magic are a potent combo. Besides being the best time to recharge your crystals, full and new moons offer supercharged opportunities to manifest magic.

FULL MOONS

Full moons are legendary as the most magic-filled night of each month. Emotions and intuitions are heightened, and the curtain between realities is at its thinnest. Gratitude rituals are one of my favorites for full moon nights, as they are grounding, protective, and possibility-expanding.

Full Moon Gratitude Ritual

Write a list of 20 things you are grateful for at this moment. Don't overthink it — simply free-write things that are making your heart glow *right now* (my lists range from big joys like good health and relationships, to small joys like my favorite mug, or a lovely sunset). Place a Moonstone plus your favorite crystal(s) on top of your list, and leave overnight in the light of the full moon. ***Expect magic.***

NEW MOONS

New moons are full of fresh, possibility-filled energy. These are very magical nights for clearing out old energy, and setting intentions.

New Moon Clearing Ritual

Wave a Selenite crystal around the edges of your body, top to bottom, a few inches above your skin. Say aloud, *"I release everything that is ready to transform. I am clean and clear."* Leave the Selenite overnight in the light of the new moon. ***Expect magic***.

New Moon Manifestation Ritual

Write a list of the goals and dreams that feel most *alive* to you right now — thinking about them makes your heart beat a little (or a lot!) faster. Place one or more crystals on top of your list, and leave overnight in the light of the new moon. ***Expect magic***. *Crystal suggestions: Citrine, Clear Quartz, Emerald, Herkimer Diamond, Kunzite, Moonstone, Opal, Pyrite, Ruby, Vera Cruz Amethyst*

CRYSTAL GRIDS

Crystal gridding is the ritual of intentionally placing crystals in symmetrical patterns. Symmetry creates a balanced flow of energy — essential for manifesting — and adding your specific intention sparks a grid to life. Experiment with premade grid patterns, or create patterns from your intuition. Sacred geometry templates are a beautiful option *(sacred geometry = mathematically precise shapes to which sacred meanings are assigned)*. Social media is a wonderful source for gridding inspiration — try searching the #crystalgrid hashtag.

To get you started, I'm sharing four of my favorite crystal grid rituals with you. These cover important basics: love, protection, manifestation, and energy clearing.

Crystal grids can be created for a limitless variety of purposes; if you can imagine it, you can create a grid to help manifest it!

Love Spell

YOU ARE SO LOVED. This grid serves two purposes: to magnify the love *you receive from others,* while also magnifying the love *you show to yourself.* You are so deserving of love — let this ritual help manifest a supercharged love vibration. Rose Quartz is a classic choice for the center crystal, but any crystal that makes your heart glow is perfect. This is a magical grid to create under your bed; don't worry about being perfectly symmetrical when placing the crystals, just do your best. Gridding your bed will create a heavenly love-bubble for you to sleep in (and indulge in other love-related activities, too!).

CRYSTALS

- 8 Clear Quartz points
- 4 Rose Quartz
- 4 Heart-chakra crystals (your choice)
- 1 Center crystal (your choice)

RITUAL

1) Cleanse crystals using your favorite method.
2) Place the center crystal in middle of grid.
3) Place the 8 Clear Quartz, points facing in.
4) Place the 4 Rose Quartz.
5) Place the 4 heart chakra crystals.
6) Take the center crystal in both hands, and hold to your heart chakra (middle of chest). Close your eyes, and take three calm, belly breaths.
7) Say aloud: *"I am so worthy of love. I surround myself with loving people. I only allow myself to be treated in loving ways. True love flows to me, through me, and all around me. I am unconditionally loved. I Am Love."*
8) Place the affirmation-infused crystal back in center of grid, and leave grid assembled for around 24 hours (if gridding under bed, leave as long as you wish).
9) When ready to dissemble, audibly say *"Thank You"* to each crystal as you remove it.
10) All the crystals are now supercharged love talismans: place the center crystal somewhere you'll see it often, and / or carry it with you regularly if it isn't delicate. Any time you need a powerful love-boost, hold it to your heart and repeat the affirmation. The other crystals can be used in a multitude of ways, just follow your intuition (*tip: place the crystals in your bathwater to create a full-body love infusion.*)

Safe + Sound

ANGELS SURROUND YOU. This ritual creates a powerful grid around anything needing an extra dose of protection: people, animals, plants, objects, and situations. You'll need to choose a crystal or crystals to represent what you're protecting. For example, if your family is going on vacation and you wish to call in extra protection while you travel, choose a crystal to represent each person. Assemble the grid before you leave, and disassemble it after you return from your trip — it's like angelic travel insurance! If you create this grid to protect someone else, it can be very special to gift them the crystal you choose to represent them. For instance, if your friend has an illness or hardship, create this grid with them represented by a center crystal, keep assembled for a few days to fully charge, and then gift the crystal to your friend as a powerful protection talisman.

CRYSTALS + TOOLS

- 4 Clear Quartz points
- 4 Selenite wands
- 4 Angelite crystals*
- 4 Black or gray crystals
- Center crystal(s) of choice
- Herbal smoke (palo santo, incense, herbs, etc) and lighter

RITUAL

1) Cleanse crystals using your favorite method.
2) Arrange Selenite wands in a square.
3) Place the crystals that represent what you're protecting into the center of the Selenite square. As you place each crystal, say aloud: *"Safe And Sound."*
4) Place the 4 black / gray crystals at corners of the square. These act as protective guardians.
5) Place the 4 Clear Quartz, points facing out. These direct negative energies away.
6) Place the 4 Angelite by each side of square. These seal the grid with angelic protection.
7) Light herbal smoke, and circle it above the grid 7 times. Say aloud: *"Angels Surround You."*
8) Your grid is now sealed and secure. Keep assembled for as long as its protection is needed.
9) When ready to dissemble, audibly say *"Thank You"* to each crystal as you remove it.

*(*If you don't own Angelite, you can use any combination of crystals that have a special connection to the angelic realm. Ideas: Amethyst, Calcite, Celestite, Golden Healer Quartz, Moonstone, Rutilated Quartz, Vera Cruz Amethyst.)*

Let It Go

RELEASE IT. When one door closes another *always* opens, but we can get so stuck trying to force open the old door that we don't notice the new one that's wide-open for us to fly through. For a powerful refresh and restart, use this grid to help you release something (or someone) holding you back. I keep this grid assembled and ready-to-go; whenever I get stuck on something, onto the grid it goes. Super-effective for releasing and moving on from things big and small. *Let it GO!*

CRYSTALS + TOOLS

• 4 Clear Quartz points
• 4 Smoky Quartz, tumbled or points
• 1 Amethyst
• Salt (Pink Himalayan is my favorite)
• Dish / paper + pen / toilet

RITUAL

1) Cleanse crystals using your favorite method.
2) Fill the dish with a layer of salt.
3) Write down what you're letting go of. Make it as detailed or simple as you wish. Fold the paper, and place in center of salt.
4) Place the Amethyst on top of paper.
5) Place the 4 Clear Quartz, points facing out.
6) Place the 4 Smoky Quartz (points facing out if they have points).
7) Take 3 deep belly breaths: imagine you're inhaling sparkling light through your nose, and exhaling gray clouds through your mouth. Shake your hands vigorously as you breathe — shake it all out! If you feel emotions, allow them to flow freely.
8) Leave grid assembled for around 24 hours.
9) When it's time, remove the paper and tear into tiny shreds. Repeat with each tear: *"I release (name / situation). I am cleansed and cleared. I Am Released!"* Pour the shreds and salt into the toilet, and flush it all away!*
10) Rub your hands together vigorously for a moment to reset your energy. Allow any emotions to flow until you feel complete.
11) Go outside if possible (or open a window). Stand strong, feet firmly balanced on the ground. Face the sun if it's visible. Place both hands on your heart, and take one giant inhale / exhale. Give your hands a final shake to release any energy stragglers.

*(*If you wish to keep the grid set up, only flush away the paper shreds plus a pinch of salt, not all the salt.)*

Trust Fund

GROW YOUR TRUST FUND. I bet you think this is a grid for getting more money, right? Actually, it's even better — this ritual is all about growing your *true* Trust Fund, aka your trust in divine timing, serendipitous flow, and magical miracles. Cycles come and go. Your job is to *stay in the mindset of expansion, gratitude, generosity, and trust.* This grid will help you stop blocking Divine Flow with anxiety, worry, and fear-fueled Doing. Trust that there's a Divine Plan running the show — God / Goddess / Source Energy / Universal Flow *(whichever your preferred term)* doesn't make mistakes!

Keeping this grid set up is a fantastic way to easily tap into your Trust Fund. Try starting each morning with steps 6 through 8; it takes just a moment, and will set a powerful vibration for the rest of your day.

CRYSTALS + TOOLS
- 4 Clear Quartz points
- 4 Pyrite
- 4 Manifestation crystals*
- Candle + matches

RITUAL
1) Cleanse crystals using your favorite method.
2) Place unlit candle in center of grid.
3) Place the 4 Pyrite on each side of the candle.
4) Place the 4 manifestation crystals on the outside of each Pyrite.
5) Place the 4 Clear Quartz points between each Pyrite, points facing out.
6) Put your feet flat on the ground, and take 3 calm breaths to ground yourself.
7) Light the candle, and say aloud: *"I am held by the universe. I am surrounded by infinite blessings and miracles. All that I need always shows up. Everything is flowing perfectly, at the right time, and in the right way for all involved. I Trust Divine Flow."*
8) Leave the candle burning for as long as you wish. If / when you blow it out, audibly say *"I trust."*
9) When ready to dissemble, audibly say *"Thank You"* to each crystal as you remove it.

*(*Choose any crystals that make you feel connected to unlimited abundance. Pictured: Herkimer Diamond / Vera Cruz Amethyst / Brandberg Amethyst / Kunzite.)*

CRYSTALS + HOLIDAYS

Holidays = holy days. Holidays are perfect opportunities to intentionally connect with crystals, as they're already set apart from the bustle of everyday life for a specific focus. Crystals can help magnify the magic of each holiday, and nurture your connection with the natural world and changing seasons. My favorite ways to crystallize holidays are wearing aligned jewelry, carrying small tumbled stones, taking a bath with crystals, and placing crystals on my nightstand on holiday nights. Holidays are also special days to gift loved ones (or yourself!) with a crystal, as it will forever be supercharged with the spirit of the holiday on which it was gifted.

VALENTINE'S DAY *Love yourself.* Be your own Valentine by making this a day to focus on self-care and self-love. Nurture your sweet heart with heart-centered crystals: *Calcite (Cobalto / Mangano), Danburite, Himalayan Samadhi Quartz, Kunzite, Morganite, Rhodochrosite, Rhodonite, Rose Quartz.*

SPRING EQUINOX (March 21/22) *Spring to life.* This equinox is all about new beginnings, fertile abundance, and fresh starts. Revitalize and re-energize with: *Aventurine, Carnelian, Chrysoprase, Emerald, Fuchsite, Garnet, Hematite Quartz, Peridot, Serpentine.*

MOTHER'S DAY *Goddess has your back.* Connect with Divine Feminine energies on your special day, Mama. Nurture yourself with: *Calcite, Chrysocolla, Garnet, Himalayan Samadhi Quartz, Kunzite, Moonstone, Morganite, Pearl, Rhodochrosite, Silver, Unakite.*

SUMMER SOLSTICE (June 21/22) *Hello, Sunshine!* Harness the power-packed energy of the longest day of the year with sunshine crystals: *Amber, Carnelian, Citrine, Copper, Gold, Golden Healer Quartz, Pyrite, Rutilated Quartz, Sunstone.*

AUTUMN EQUINOX (September 21/22)
Embrace your dark side. Connect to your
Shadow Self (the parts of yourself difficult to
accept) on this day marking the centerpoint
of the change from light to dark. Bravely
mine your shadows for soul-gold with:
*Agate, Amethyst, Aragonite, Azurite,
Brandberg Amethyst, Labradorite, Smoky
Quartz, Tiger's Eye, Tourmaline Quartz.*

SAMHAIN (October 31) *Beyond the veil.*
The veils between worlds grow thin on this
mystical day. Pay homage to loved ones
who have passed to the other side, and
connect to the wisdom of ancestors with
crystals for connecting to the spirit world:
*Amethyst, Charoite, Epidote, Labradorite,
Lapis Lazuli, Lodolite, Opal, Obsidian.*

THANKSGIVING *Practice gratitude.*
Take a moment on this holiday of feasting
to give gratitude to Mother Earth for
all she provides, with: *Amber, Aventurine,
Bloodstone, Chrysoprase, Epidote,
Fuchsite, Jasper (Kambaba), Ruby Fuchsite,
Serpentine, Turquoise, Unakite.*

WINTER SOLSTICE (December 21/22)
Get crystal clear. The darkest day of the
year holds space for deep rest and mindful
introspection. Go quiet and get clear with:
*Apophyllite, Calcite (Optical), Clear Quartz,
Iolite, Jet, Labradorite, Scolecite, Selenite,
Smoky Quartz.*

WINTER HOLIDAYS

Part 1: *Devotion.* Winter holidays from
many traditions share celebratory gratitude
for divine blessings. Connect to devotional
gratitude with angelic crystals: *Angelite,
Calcite, Celestite, Golden Healer Quartz,
Herkimer Diamond, Himalayan Samadhi
Quartz, Kunzite, Rutilated Quartz,
Vera Cruz Amethyst.*

Part 2: *Ground yourself.* Family time and
holiday travel can both be intense. To help
you stay centered and protected, carry one
or more of these crystals somewhere on
your body as you travel for holidays, and
while you interact with challenging relatives:
*Bloodstone, Hematite, Jasper, Obsidian,
Ruby Zoisite, Scolecite, Serpentine,
Smoky Quartz, Tourmaline (Black).*

NEW YEAR *New Year = New You.* Release
outdated energies weighing you down, and
start the new year with fresh energy and
inspiration with crystals for cleansing,
clarity, and vision: *Amethyst, Apatite,
Apophyllite, Aquamarine, Brandberg
Amethyst, Calcite (Optical), Clear Quartz,
Halite, Herkimer Diamond, Kyanite,
Lemurian Quartz, Sapphire, Selenite,
Smoky Quartz, Topaz.*

*(Note: if you're located in the Southern Hemisphere,
flip the dates of the equinoxes and solstices.)*

CRYSTALS + GIFTS

Although I may be just a *bit* biased, I really do think that crystals are one of the best things to give or receive — they truly are gifts that keep on giving! Here are my favorites for a variety of occasions.

BIRTHDAY
Agate, Amethyst, Apophyllite, Calcite, Celestite, Citrine, Clear Quartz, Fluorite, Golden Healer Quartz, Herkimer Diamond, Jasper, Rose Quartz, Spirit Quartz, Vera Cruz Amethyst

CONGRATULATIONS
Citrine, Clear Quartz, Gold, Herkimer Diamond, Pyrite, Rose Quartz, Ruby, Spirit Quartz, Vera Cruz Amethyst

GRADUATION
Amazonite, Aventurine, Calcite (Optical), Celestite, Chrysoprase, Citrine, Clear Quartz, Emerald, Jasper, Pyrite, Ruby, Sunstone, Vera Cruz Amethyst

NEW JOB
Amazonite, Aventurine, Chrysoprase, Citrine, Clear Quartz, Emerald, Fluorite, Jade, Pyrite, Sunstone

BRIDAL SHOWER
Apophyllite, Celestite, Clear Quartz, Himalayan Samadhi Quartz, Moonstone, Rose Quartz

WEDDING
Amethyst, Apophyllite, Celestite, Clear Quartz, Kyanite, Rose Quartz, Selenite, Smoky Quartz

NEW HOME
Amethyst, Aventurine, Apophyllite, Citrine, Clear Quartz, Pyrite, Rose Quartz, Selenite, Serpentine, Spirit Quartz, Smoky Quartz, Tourmaline (Black)

BABY SHOWER
Agate (Blue Lace), Angelite, Amethyst, Apophyllite, Calcite (Mangano), Celestite, Chalcedony, Clear Quartz, Lepidolite, Rose Quartz, Spirit Quartz

NEW PARENT
Carnelian, Celestite, Garnet, Gold, Hematite Quartz, Jasper (Red), Lepidolite, Moonstone, Pearl, Rose Quartz, Ruby

GET WELL
Amber, Calcite (all), Carnelian, Citrine, Emerald, Fuchsite, Golden Healer Quartz, Hematite Quartz, Jasper (Red), Rose Quartz, Ruby (all)

BROKEN HEART
Calcite (Cobalto, Mangano), Danburite, Garnet, Himalayan Samadhi Quartz, Kunzite, Morganite, Rhodochrosite, Rhodonite, Rose Quartz, Ruby, Unakite

GRIEF
Ammonite, Angelite, Celestite, Clear Quartz, Desert Rose, Jasper, Obsidian (Apache Tear), Petrified Wood, Rhodonite, Rose Quartz, Smoky Quartz, Tourmaline (Black), Unakite

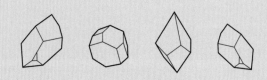

Crystal Apothecary

What do you wish to manifest? What do you wish to release?

I know the abundance of crystal varieties can feel overwhelming, especially if you're new to crystal healing. Welcome to my crystal apothecary! Here are my 10 go-to crystals for a wide variety of remedies. Explore the profiles of the crystals in each prescription, and use your intuition to choose the best combination for you.

Very important: please don't feel limited to only the crystals listed — these prescriptions are meant to be a launchpad to spark your own intuition.

Dear Universe, More of this, please!

I wish to feel MORE...

ABUNDANT
Aventurine, Citrine, Clear Quartz, Emerald, Gold, Jade, Peridot, Pyrite, Ruby, Vera Cruz Amethyst

BOUNDARIED
Agate, Bloodstone, Hematite, Jasper (Dragon's Blood/Leopardskin), Obsidian, Pyrite, Ruby, Tiger's Eye, Tourmaline (Black), Vanadinite

BRAVE
Agate, Aragonite, Bloodstone, Jasper (Dragon's Blood/Red), Garnet, Gold, Obsidian, Ruby, Tourmaline (Black), Turquoise

CALM
Agate (Blue Lace), Aquamarine, Calcite (Blue/Caribbean/Mangano), Celestite, Chalcedony, Howlite, Larimar, Pearl, Scolecite, Sodalite

CLARITY
Amethyst (all), Apophyllite, Azurite, Calcite (Optical), Clear Quartz, Herkimer Diamond, Iolite, Labradorite, Selenite, Tanzanite

CONFIDENT
Agate, Carnelian, Chrysocolla, Citrine, Gold, Jade, Jasper (Bumblebee/Mookaite/Yellow), Peridot, Pyrite, Sunstone

CREATIVE
Ametrine, Citrine, Clear Quartz, Fluorite, Herkimer Diamond, Lemurian Quartz, Lodolite, Moldavite, Peacock Ore, Pyrite

ENERGETIC
Carnelian, Citrine, Copper, Garnet, Gold, Hematite Quartz, Peridot, Pyrite, Ruby, Rutilated Quartz

EXPRESSIVE
Amazonite, Aquamarine, Chrysocolla, Kyanite, Lapis Lazuli, Ruby Kyanite, Sapphire, Sodalite, Topaz (Blue/Green), Turquoise

FERTILE
Carnelian, Chrysocolla, Emerald, Garnet, Hematite Quartz, Jasper (Red), Moonstone, Pearl, Ruby, Silver

FOCUSED
Calcite (Optical), Desert Rose, Fluorite, Galena, Hematite, Jet, Obsidian, Pyrite, Selenite, Vanadinite

GROUNDED
Copper, Desert Rose, Garnet, Gold, Hematite, Jasper (all), Pyrite, Ruby, Smoky Quartz, Tourmaline (Black)

HAPPY
Aura Quartz, Calcite (Cobalto), Citrine, Clear Quartz, Kunzite, Opal (Common), Rutilated Quartz, Spirit Quartz, Tourmaline (Colored), Vera Cruz Amethyst.

HEALTHY
Amber, Calcite (all), Carnelian, Citrine, Emerald, Fuchsite, Golden Healer Quartz, Hematite Quartz, Jasper (Red), Ruby (all).

HOPEFUL
Amethyst (all), Apophyllite, Celestite, Clear Quartz, Diamond, Kunzite, Moonstone, Morganite, Rose Quartz, Spirit Quartz

INSPIRED
Amethyst (all), Apophyllite, Celestite, Clear Quartz, Golden Healer Quartz, Herkimer Diamond, Himalayan Samadhi Quartz, Sapphire, Spirit Quartz, Topaz

LOVED
Calcite (Cobalto/Mangano), Danburite, Himalayan Samadhi Quartz, Kunzite, Morganite, Rhodochrosite, Rose Quartz, Stilbite, Topaz (Pink), Tourmaline (Colored)

LUCKY
Aventurine, Chrysoprase, Citrine, Emerald, Jade, Kunzite, Opal (Precious), Pyrite, Ruby, Vera Cruz Amethyst

MAGICAL
Amethyst (all), Bloodstone, Charoite, Clear Quartz, Epidote, Herkimer Diamond, Kunzite, Moldavite, Moonstone, Opal (Precious)

PEACEFUL
Angelite, Apophyllite, Calcite (Blue/Mangano), Celestite, Chalcedony, Danburite, Howlite, Rose Quartz, Scolecite, Stilbite

POWERFUL
Diamond, Emerald, Gold, Jade, Pyrite, Ruby, Sapphire, Tiger's Eye, Tourmaline (Black), Vanadinite

PROTECTED
Agate, Amethyst, Angelite, Bloodstone, Garnet, Jasper, Obsidian, Ruby, Tourmaline (Black), Turquoise

SMART
Calcite (Optical), Chrysoprase, Citrine, Clear Quartz, Fluorite, Galena, Iolite, Jade, Pyrite, Vanadinite

SPIRITUAL
Amethyst (all), Apophyllite, Celestite, Clear Quartz, Golden Healer Quartz, Herkimer Diamond, Himalayan Samadhi Quartz, Lapis Lazuli, Sapphire, Topaz

TURNED ON
Carnelian, Citrine, Emerald, Garnet, Gold, Hematite Quartz, Jasper (Red), Moonstone, Ruby, Tangerine Quartz

WILLPOWER
Apatite, Carnelian, Diamond, Gold, Jade, Malachite, Peridot, Pyrite, Ruby, Vanadinite

Help! I really need support

I wish to feel LESS...

ADDICTED
Amethyst (all, especially Brandberg), Apatite, Carnelian, Malachite, Pearl, Pyrite, Rose Quartz, Ruby, Smoky Quartz, Tourmaline (Black)

ANGRY
Agate (Blue Lace), Calcite (Blue), Chalcedony, Howlite, Larimar, Lepidolite, Moonstone, Scolecite, Silver, Smoky Quartz

ANXIOUS
Calcite (all, especially Blue/Mangano), Celestite, Chalcedony, Jasper, Hematite, Howlite, Lepidolite, Pearl, Rose Quartz, Scolecite

DEPRESSED
Amethyst (all), Citrine, Clear Quartz, Kunzite, Lepidolite, Lithium Quartz, Rose Quartz, Ruby, Rutilated Quartz, Spirit Quartz

EXHAUSTED
Calcite (Red), Carnelian, Citrine, Copper, Garnet, Hematite Quartz, Jasper (Red), Ruby, Rutilated Quartz, Tangerine Quartz

GRIEF
Ammonite, Desert Rose, Jasper, Obsidian (Apache Tear), Petrified Wood, Rhodonite, Rose Quartz, Smoky Quartz, Tourmaline (Black), Unakite

HEARTBROKEN
Calcite (Cobalto/Mangano), Danburite, Garnet, Kunzite, Lepidolite, Morganite, Rhodochrosite, Rhodonite, Rose Quartz, Unakite

INDECISIVE
Brandberg Amethyst, Calcite (Optical), Clear Quartz, Gold, Iolite, Jet, Obsidian (Rainbow/Sheen), Pyrite, Tanzanite, Vanadinite

INSOMNIA
Agate (Blue Lace), Amethyst, Celestite, Chalcedony (Blue), Howlite, Lepidolite, Moonstone, Pearl, Scolecite, Tourmaline (Black)

JEALOUS
Ametrine, Clear Quartz, Howlite, Jasper (Mookaite), Lithium Quartz, Pearl, Pyrite, Rose Quartz, Serpentine, Spirit Quartz

LONELY
Agate (Dendritic/Moss/Tree), Amber, Danburite, Kunzite, Morganite, Opal (Dendritic), Rhodochrosite, Rose Quartz, Spirit Quartz, Tourmaline (Colored)

OVERWHELMED
Celestite, Danburite, Hematite, Jasper (all, especially Kambaba/Rainforest), Jet, Larimar, Obsidian, Rhodonite, Rose Quartz, Unakite

RESENTFUL
Apophyllite, Celestite, Clear Quartz, Howlite, Lithium Quartz, Malachite, Rose Quartz, Ruby (all), Serpentine, Sunstone

SCARCITY
Agate (Dendritic/Moss/Tree), Aventurine, Citrine, Diamond, Emerald, Gold, Herkimer Diamond, Jade, Pyrite, Ruby

SCARED
Agate, Angelite, Bloodstone, Celestite, Garnet, Gold, Jasper (Dragon's Blood/Leopardskin/Red), Obsidian, Ruby, Tourmaline (Black)

SICK
Amber, Calcite (all), Carnelian, Citrine, Emerald, Fuchsite, Golden Healer Quartz, Hematite Quartz, Jasper (Red), Ruby (all)

STRESSED
Azurite, Calcite (Blue/Caribbean), Celestite, Howlite, Jasper, Larimar, Lepidolite, Smoky Quartz, Tourmaline (Black), Turquoise

STUCK
Amethyst (all), Chrysoprase, Citrine, Clear Quartz, Herkimer Diamond, Kyanite, Moldavite, Pyrite, Smoky Quartz, Tanzanite

TRAUMATIZED
Amethyst (all, especially Brandberg), Calcite (all, especially Mangano), Garnet, Jasper, Rose Quartz, Ruby, Tangerine Quartz, Tiger's Eye, Tourmaline (Black), Tourmaline Quartz

WORRIED
Angelite, Aquamarine, Azurite, Celestite, Iolite, Kunzite, Labradorite, Larimar, Moonstone, Sapphire

remember:

There are as many ways to add crystal magic and healing into your daily life as there are stars in the sky, the possibilities limited only by the edges of your imagination. If there is only one thing I would wish you to gain from this book, it is the empowerment to *listen to your own inner voice.* You can read all the crystal books in the world, and get advice from the very best experts, but no one can truly know which crystal is right for you — at this exact moment in your journey — better than you, yourself. Your intuition is the way crystals will speak directly to you, for your unique circumstances and healing. **Listen to your crystals.**

Widening the lens, this also means that there is no one who truly knows what is best for you *in any circumstance* than you, yourself. Your intuition is your most valuable magic; always listen to it, always trust it. Stand in your power. There is true magic within you. **Listen to yourself.**

Trust your magic.

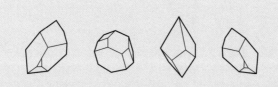

The Crystals

⊛ Primary **color** variations
⊙ Largest modern **source(s)**
⊰ **Chakra(s)** crystal resonates with
♡ **Special care** recommendations
◊ Whether **water exposure** causes damage

Magic = Metaphysical qualities

Notes = Practical information

Affirmation = Activates a connection between you and your crystal. Repeat aloud or silently, whenever your intuition guides you.

This section is meant to be used as both a traditional reference guide, and as an intuitive crystal oracle. Like pulling an oracle card, this is a magical way to receive a message you need to hear, be guided in the right direction, and connect to support from your guides, angels, and intuition.

CRYSTAL ORACLE

Close your eyes.
Take 3 slow, calm breaths.
Intuitively open to a crystal profile.

The crystal you open to
holds magic for you.

Agate

PROTECTION • COURAGE • STRENGTH

✳ **Color** All shades of the rainbow

◉ **Born in** Worldwide

♋ **Chakras** Varies according to color

◊ **Water Cleansing** ☒ Y ☐ N

MAGIC Agate is a protective mineral with ancient stories to tell. This banded gemstone has been carved into holy objects and magic amulets since first discovered, thousands of years ago, on the banks of the Sicilian river Achates. Legends have long whispered that Agate can grant magical powers of invisibility and courage. *Invisibility = much more than just what meets the eye.* Agate is a crystal to keep close when you feel vulnerable or in need of extra protection and courage, both in body and soul. Although your journey through life will hold many moments for shining brightly in the spotlight, it will also offer equally important opportunities for walking bravely through shadows, both external and internal. Agate, with its mix of brightly translucent and darkly opaque layers, reminds us that being a true magic-maker requires stepping bravely into both situations — the light *and* the dark — and will help support *and* protect you along the many turns in your journey.

NOTES Agate is found worldwide in a vast array of colors, often named after the source location *(pictured: Laguna Agate from Ojo Laguna, Mexico, a rare variety valued for its beautiful colors)*. A striped variety of the mineral Chalcedony, a 'true' Agate has curved or concentric bands that are both opaque and translucent; however, the name is used loosely in the crystal healing world, and there are many 'Agates' that don't meet those specifications. Brightly colored Agates with only a color name (e.g. Pink Agate) are usually artificially dyed. Turn the page to explore popular varieties. *(aah-git)*

AFFIRMATION

"I am protected and supported, always and everywhere"

AGATE VARIETIES:

1) BLUE LACE AGATE The most soothing and calming Agate variety, a lullaby encapsulated in a crystal. These blue and white striped stones are wonderful for calming anxiety and hyperactivity, and very soothing for children.
Chakras: Throat, Crown

2) BOTSWANA AGATE These banded crystals are classic Agates, and hold the magic described on page 84, with an added boost of heart-nurturing energy. Comes in several color variations. The most common variety has bands of gray, pink, and white. **Apricot Agate** is an alternative name for the orange-pink and white variety.
Chakras: Root, Sacral, Heart

3) CRAZY LACE AGATE Throw off the shackles of conformity and dance to your own unique beat! Helps you step into being your authentic, one-of-a-kind self, and have much more fun on your journey. An intricately patterned variety, with multicolored swirls going every direction.
Chakras: All

4) DENDRITIC AGATE This is a crystal for when you crave the grounding, nurturing feeling you get from spending time in nature. Reminds you that everything is interconnected, and you can trust that you will always be supported and nurtured — you are safely held in the web of life. Translucent white-gray with fernlike inclusions of black, brown, and gray.
Chakras: Root, Heart. (den-drih-tik)

5) FIRE AGATE Helps light your inner soul-fire, energizing you to confidently move forward on your biggest dreams and goals. Translucent reddish-brown with internal multicolored iridescence.
Chakras: Root, Sacral

6) FLOWER AGATE This is a variety for all you cottagecore romantics! Helps your sensitive, beauty-loving soul feel nourished and nurtured. Translucent gray-brown with multicolored pastel inclusions. *Chakra: Heart*

7) GRAPE AGATE Helps you channel inspiration and spiritual guidance with a joyful sense of bubbly lightness. A unique variety that forms in clusters of tiny purple spheres, resembling bunches of grapes. *Chakras: Crown, 3rd Eye*

8) IRIS AGATE A rare variety which shows rainbow iridescence when held up to light. A beautiful reminder that the universe is filled with magic — your job is to trust and receive. Get out of the way and allow magic to manifest! *Chakra: Crown*

9) MOSS AGATE The translucent variety of green Dendritic Agate, has the same metaphysical qualities. Clear with primarily green inclusions. *Chakras: Root, Heart.*

10) TREE AGATE The opaque variety of green Dendritic Agate, has the same metaphysical qualities (see above). White with primarily green inclusions.
Chakras: Root, Heart.

1

2

3

4

5

6

7

8

9

10

(Note: there is much overlap between what is sold as Moss Agate vs. Tree Agate, as they have the same mineral composition.)

Amazonite

TRUTH-TELLING • FLOW • COURAGE

✳ **Color** Shimmery blue-green

◉ **Born in** Brazil, USA, Russia, Madagascar

❧ **Chakras** Throat

💧 **Water Cleansing** ☒ Y ☐ N

MAGIC *Share your truth.* Are you ready to be a courageous truth-teller? Let Amazonite be your guide. Like the mighty river after which this shimmering crystal is named, Amazonite is a crystal of strength, flow, and power, inspiring you to dive deep into your soul to unearth the shining truths hidden within. Whether you're a teacher, writer, singer, or anyone who uses their voice to make an impact, Amazonite is a valuable crystal ally that can help you communicate with confidence and authenticity. The next time you're facing a big presentation, interview, or audition, hold Amazonite up to your throat and repeat its empowering affirmation. And for those times when you need in-the-moment inspiration and support, tuck a small piece into your clothing, or wear Amazonite jewelry. An essential crystal for all you social media mavens who feel led to inspire and uplift with your content, Amazonite will help you bravely post and share from your higher self, for a light-filled social media presence. *Less aspiration, more inspiration.* Because as we encourage others to fly, we ourselves are lifted higher. When we bravely share our own truth, we create a ripple effect of courageous honesty. Let Amazonite help you share your authentic truth, so we can all soar together!

NOTES Amazonite is in the feldspar family (Labradorite and Moonstone are its better-known cousins). It generally forms in non-crystallized masses and is sold as small raw or polished pieces, although tabular crystal formations are possible. Specimens embedded with Smoky Quartz or Black Tourmaline have an added boost of grounding energy. Also called **Amazon Jade** and **Amazon Stone**. *(ah-muh-zuh-nite)*

AFFIRMATION
"I bravely share my truth"

Amber

ANCESTRAL HEALING • FOLKLORIC MAGIC • IMMUNE BOOST

⊛ **Color** Shades of honey

◎ **Born in** Baltic Sea Region,
Dominican Republic

⬡ **Chakras** Sacral, Heart, Solar Plexus

◊ **Water Cleansing** ☒ Y ☐ N

MAGIC Amber is a gem of ancient forest magic and old-world fairytales. Born from the 'blood' of prehistoric pine trees, these organic gemstones are fossilized drops of resin that have been smoothed and polished by saltwater waves over millions of years. This can be a particularly meaningful talisman for those with ancestral roots in Eastern Europe, the Baltics, and the Dominican Republic, where Amber has been used for ritual, adornment, and healing since the earliest humans. Spend time with this honey-colored fossil to connect with the myths and folklore of your ancestors, and to awaken the indigenous magic and wisdom that runs deep within your core. To connect with Amber, spend time with a piece on your sacral chakra *(low stomach)* to release inherited ancestral karmas; on your solar plexus chakra *(navel)* for a burst of sunshine vitality and healing; and on your heart chakra *(chest)* to wrap your immune system and heart in a giant, warm-honey hug. Beautiful Amber jewelry comes in all shapes and sizes, and is a wonderful way to keep this crystal's vibration close.

NOTES The Baltic coast is by far the largest Amber source, as about 90% of gem-quality pieces are found there. **Copal** is organic resin that is much younger than Amber. Amber can hold a slight electrical charge: rub it on your palm for about a minute and then hold it near a piece of hair. Genuine Amber should attract the hair with static electricity (note: plastic and glass imitations are extremely common). And look closely: Amber can have prehistoric insects and plant matter trapped inside!

AFFIRMATION
"The wisdom of my ancestors flows through me"

Amethyst

TRANSFORMATION • PROTECTION • REST

✳ **Color** Shades of violet

◉ **Born in** Brazil, Uruguay, worldwide

❀ **Chakras** Crown

♡ **Care** Fades in direct sunlight

◊ **Water Cleansing** ☒ Y ☐ N

MAGIC Full of regal coloring and radiant sparkle, Amethyst is a crystal of transformation. A gemstone of many legends and lineages, ultra-popular Amethyst is the star of our modern crystal renaissance. And why is Amethyst so popular right now — why are crystals, overall, so popular right now? I believe it is because *we are the new ones*. We are transcending and healing intergenerational traumas, rewiring ourselves to be reborn in a new way of being. And Amethyst strengthens our connection to the *miracle* of our existence. Because each of us are the result of an infinite number of intergenerational miracles — care and support, sexual ecstasy, lucky breaks, and unconditional love. Let Amethyst help you operate from the miracles and love in your ancestral line, rather than the trauma.

A beloved crystal for sleep issues, Amethyst also helps switch off your fight-or-flight motor, allowing you to access deep rest. So rest, magic maker. Rest now, so the generations upon generations of ancestral energy in your nervous system can dissolve, transform, transcend. *Rewire yourself*.

NOTES Amethyst is the violet variety of Quartz. Once as expensive as diamonds, today Amethyst is found worldwide in a variety of geological environments. The majority of beautiful clusters are pieces of geodes from Brazil and Uruguay, formed from gas bubbles trapped in volcanic lava flows. **Green Amethyst (Prasiolite)** is heat-treated to create its green color. **Pink Amethyst** is a variety of Hematite Quartz *(see page 158)*. Amethyst is a February birthstone.

AFFIRMATION
"I am a miracle"

Ametrine

CREATIVITY • INTUITION • MANIFESTATION

- ✳ **Color** Violet + orange
- ⊘ **Born in** Bolivia, Brazil
- ☊ **Chakras** Sacral, Solar Plexus, Crown
- ♡ **Care** Fades in direct sunlight
- ◊ **Water Cleansing** ☒ Y ☐ N

MAGIC The cosmic love child of Amethyst and Citrine, Ametrine is a crystal for dance-to-your-own-beat creativity. This violet-orange gemstone is all about taking charge of your own life, and staying true to your intuition. Ametrine helps you commit to living a magical life filled with things from your 'must' list, instead of things from other people's 'should' lists. *Throw off the shackles of conformity and embrace your magnificent, beyond-the-ordinary dreams and visions!* The combination of Citrine's motivational skills with Amethyst's transformative vibration makes Ametrine a great partner for anyone who needs help sticking to goals, clearing bad habits, and kicking addictions. Try drinking an Ametrine elixir *(see page 47)* to help you stay on track with health and wellness goals, sleep with one under your pillow for dreamtime support, and keep one within view while working or studying for an extra zap of creativity and inspiration. This beautiful crystal is especially helpful for those in fields that involve merging inspiration with action, such as coaches and mindful business owners. Ametrine = follow *your* dreams!

NOTES Ametrine is usually primarily purple, with smaller sections of orange. A rarer crystal, Bolivia is the main source of natural Ametrine. Specimens from other localities are commonly heat-treated to enhance their orange color, however I find that heat-treated Ametrine has essentially the same metaphysical energies as natural. *(am-uh-treen)*

AFFIRMATION
"I am manifesting my dreams"

Ammonite

TRUST • GROWTH • EMBRACE CHANGE

⊛ **Color** Shades of brown, iridescent

◉ **Born in** Madagascar, Morocco, worldwide

⚘ **Chakras** Root, Sacral, Solar Plexus

◊ **Water Cleansing** ☒ Y ☐ N

MAGIC Ammonite, a fossilized mineral shaped like a spiral, can teach us a thing or two about embracing the twists and turns of life. When you hold one in your hand, you're not only holding something that could have lived as long ago as 450 million years (!), you're holding a reminder of the cyclical nature of life, and the transformative power of evolution. Ammonite's spiral shape symbolizes the ever-changing journey we all experience; the ups and downs, the twists and turns, the moments of joy and the moments of pain. Life isn't about taking two steps forward and one step back (as the popular saying goes) but a spiral; yes, you will circle around and come back to familiar places, but always with new knowledge and understanding. You are always evolving. *Life is a spiral*. So the next time you feel lost or

overwhelmed, take a deep breath, and hold your Ammonite close. Let this ancient fossil help you remember to embrace the spiral, and welcome every change and turn with open arms, trusting that each experience — no matter how challenging — is part of the journey towards your greatest growth and transformation.

NOTES Ammonites are the fossilized shells of cephalopods, sea creatures that lived millions of years ago. Medieval Europeans thought that Ammonites were fossilized coiled snakes, and considered them to have special healing powers. Ammonites can be found all over the planet in a variety of colors, iridescence, and sizes. **Ammolite** is a gemstone made from colorful, iridescent Ammonites. *(aah-muh-nite)*

AFFIRMATION
"I trust the spiral"

Angelite

ANGELIC PROTECTION • GUIDANCE • PEACE

❀ **Color** Opaque powder blue
⊘ **Born in** Peru
🜂 **Chakras** Throat, Crown
◊ **Water Cleansing** ☐ Y ☒ N

MAGIC It's easy to remember the magic of this heavenly crystal: *Angel + Light = Angelite.* Angelite is a crystal for connecting with angelic guidance, protection, and inspiration. We each have a heavenly team surrounding us at all times, our own posse of angels walking alongside us at every step. Angelite is a reminder that you are never, ever alone, and is one of the best crystals to use for soothing anxiety, loneliness, and fear. Keep a piece tucked into your clothing or pocket to help you feel safe while out and about, and place one under your pillow for dreamtime protection and guidance. This is a wonderful crystal for children, as it can help them feel safe and secure: put a crystal in a child's bedroom to create a soothing oasis of peace and calm (Angelite makes a wonderful gift for new parents). Blending the healing vibrations of the throat and crown chakras, Angelite gently reminds your overwhelmed self that you don't need to figure everything out on your own; all you need to do is ask your angels for help, and they're right there, always and forever by your side.

NOTES Angelite is a metaphysical name used for blue, non-crystallized **Anhydrite**. Angelite forms in opaque masses and is generally sold as small polished pieces, while Anhydrite can form delicate, prismatic crystals that look like wings, a rare variety worth seeking out as it's quite special. Note: although many crystal-healing books claim Angelite is a compressed form of Celestite, this is incorrect. *(ain-gel-ite)*

AFFIRMATION
"Angels surround me"

Apatite

WILLPOWER • HEALTHY CHOICES • DETOX

✳ **Color** Teal, green, yellow
◎ **Born in** Brazil, Mexico, Madagascar
🜁 **Chakras** Solar Plexus, Throat, 3rd Eye
◌ **Water Cleansing** ☒ Y ☐ N

MAGIC *Rock Your Willpower.* Apatite is the crystal to grab whenever you need help with anything willpower-related: resolutions, healthy eating, substance avoidance, self-kindness, etc. Keep one of these little crystals within view in your kitchen to help you consistently make healthy, nourishing choices. This lovely mineral works by detoxing you from patterns and habits that aren't helpful, the deep-rooted stuff holding on from past lives and alternate realities that you definitely want to release for current-time clarity and health. Take a bath with Apatite to infuse your water with detoxifying vibrations, or try drinking an Apatite elixir *(see page 47)* for healthy infusions from the inside out. This is a great crystal for bedrooms, as it will gently work on you while you sleep. Remember: being healthy isn't a self-serving goal, as the better you feel, the better you can share your gifts and spirit with the world.

NOTES Apatite is a family of calcium-phosphate minerals and crystallizes in a variety of colors, with the opaque teal-blue variety being the most affordable. Yellow is the most common color of translucent Apatite; translucent purple, pink, and teal crystals are rare. Apatite was named after *Apate,* Greek goddess of deceit, as historically it was often mistaken for other minerals, such as Aquamarine. It is primarily mined for industrial use, as a key ingredient of fertilizer. Fun fact: your teeth and bones are built from biological Apatite! Pronounced just like 'appetite': *(aah-puh-tite).*

AFFIRMATION
"I am supported in making the best choices for my wellbeing"

Apophyllite

ENERGY FILTER • SPACE CLEARING • CONSCIOUS COMMUNICATION

✸ **Color** Clear, white, green, pink

⟳ **Born in** India

☍ **Chakras** 3rd Eye, Crown

◊ **Water Cleansing** ☒ Y ☐ N

MAGIC *Purify.* I call Apophyllite 'The Crystal Air Purifier' because this stunning crystal tirelessly toils away in the background, filtering copious amounts of energy in order to keep the surrounding space fresh, clear, and buzzing with high-vibration energy. By simply placing a cluster of Apophyllite in a bustling area like your living room or kitchen, you'll notice a remarkable shift in the energy within 24 hours. These glittering crystals are ideal for any environment that sees a constant ebb and flow of people, such as an office or store, and I think it's a must-have for healing practitioners to keep in their waiting and treatment rooms. As an added bonus, Apophyllite is a natural facilitator of *conscious communication* — communication that is honest, compassionate, and crystal clear — another reason why this is such a valuable crystal for spaces where you and your loved ones gather. A perfect gift for new marriages and new homes, Apophyllite is a true treasure for anyone who wishes to uplevel the energy within and around them.

NOTES I think Apophyllite is one of the best bang-for-your-buck crystals, because sizable clusters are more affordable than many other minerals. It usually forms as clear or white clusters, often mixed with a variety of other minerals such as Chalcedony, Stilbite, and Heulandite. Green and pink Apophyllite are rarer colors (watch out for artificially dyed clusters). Apophyllite is primarily sourced in India, gathered by miners as a byproduct of industrial mining for road material. Its pyramid-shaped tips can 'pop' off rather easily, so take care to keep your cluster's tips intact. *(ah-pah-fuh-lite)*

AFFIRMATION

"I am surrounded by the clearest + highest vibrations"

Aquamarine

FLOW • CLARITY • REJUVENATION

✳ **Color** Translucent aqua

◎ **Born in** Brazil, Madagascar, Pakistan

❀ **Chakras** Throat, 3rd Eye

♡ **Care** Fades in direct sunlight

◊ **Water Cleansing** ☒ Y ☐ N

MAGIC *Mermaid Magic.* Aquamarine is for anyone who secretly (or not so secretly) wishes they were a mermaid — because if mermaids wear jewelry, I imagine it glitters with these seafoam gems! Mermaids have allured and enchanted us humans since ancient days with their mysterious half-woman, half-fish forms. Inhabiting the liminal space between land and sea, mermaids embody 'the in-between,' the space between the known and unknown. *Magic is strongest in the in-between*, and Aquamarine has a deep connection to this mystical realm. By dissolving energy blockages that keep you stuck in your everyday routines, stale habits, and fear-based thinking, Aquamarine will help guide you to a state of flow and freedom. This blue-green gemstone helps calm overactive mental chatter and ease anxiety, so you can access crystal-clear clarity and refreshing rejuvenation. So embrace your inner mermaid with Aquamarine: let the magic of the in-between flow you to new heights and depths, and help you uncover the treasures that lie within!

NOTES Named after the Latin term for seawater, *aqua marina,* Aquamarine is the blue variety of beryl, making it a sister gem to Emerald and Morganite. It forms in long, hexagonal crystals, commonly embedded in pegmatite rock and paired with silvery mica. Gemstones are often heat-treated to turn them pure blue. Aquamarine is a March birthstone. *(ah-kwa-mah-reen)*

AFFIRMATION
"I let go + allow flow"

Aragonite

CHANGE • COURAGE • EMBRACE THE UNKNOWN

✳ **Color** Red-orange, white
◉ **Born in** Morocco, Mexico
🐾 **Chakras** Sacral, Root
💧 **Water Cleansing** ☐ Y ☒ N

MAGIC *When one door closes, another opens.* Aragonite, with its dense core radiating starry spikes in all directions, helps you stay open to a sense of adventure and curiosity as change swirls around you. Change is inevitable, something that — without any doubt — is coming down the road for all of us. Instead of clinging tightly to the past, let Aragonite help you bravely embrace the unknown and its myriad possibilities, adventures, and opportunities. This is an ideal crystal ally for times when world events and news overwhelm you, and you feel like crawling into a hole and sleeping for, oh, the next decade or so. I feel you. But these are precisely the times when *your light is needed more than ever*, my Lightworker friend. So let Aragonite help you stay engaged, grounded, and focused

on the bigger picture. Place this sacral-activating crystal on your sacral chakra *(low stomach)*, breathe calmly and deeply, and meditate on these wise words from one of our modern goddesses of sacral energy, Marilyn Monroe: *"Sometimes good things fall apart so better things can fall together."*

NOTES A calcium-based mineral, Aragonite crystallizes worldwide in a variety of shapes and colors. The variety you'll most commonly find for sale is called **Star Aragonite** or **Sputnik Aragonite**, for its resemblance to Soviet-era satellites *(pictured)*, and primarily comes from Morocco. Mexico produces beautiful, delicate clusters, usually glossy white, which are also sold under the name **Cave Calcite**. Pink Aragonite is a recent discovery (note that inexpensive specimens are often dyed pink), and blue Aragonite is commonly sold as **Caribbean Calcite** *(see page 115). (ah-rag-uh-nite)*

AFFIRMATION
"I bravely embrace the unknown"

Aura Crystals

FUN • JOY • MAGIC

⊛ **Color** Iridescent rainbow shades

⊘ **Born in** USA, China

⊗ **Chakras** Varies according to color

◊ **Water Cleansing** ☐ Y ☒ N

MAGIC Aura crystals are the fun party kids of the modern crystal revival. These rainbow-shimmer crystals first came on the scene in the '80s, and are the result of organic + human alchemy. Beginning life as natural crystals (usually a variety of Quartz), they are treated with a combination of extremely high heat and precious metal vapors, which coats them in their distinctive iridescence and saturated colors. 'Treated' crystals tend to be polarizing; some crystal lovers adore them, while others feel they're artificial and can't stand them. To each their own: if these shimmery crystals attract you, they hold magic for you! Aura crystals hold the magic of the original crystal variety plus an added sparkle of lighthearted fun and joy. *(Note: if the crystal has a colored coating, its magic aligns with its primary color; see the color chart on page 38.)*

NOTES As treated crystals are currently riding a wave of popularity, manufacturers are coating a wide variety of crystals with iridescence. If 'aura' is in a crystal's name, assume it has a human-made coating. Quality Aura crystals have a coating that cannot be scratched off; avoid cheap imitations that scratch easily, as they are coated with chemicals rather than precious metals. The specific names of Aura varieties can get confusing as there are many variations and overlaps, plus new varieties being created. Classic favorites include clear **Angel Aura** (pictured, also called **Opal Aura**), multicolored **Titanium Aura**, blue **Aqua Aura**, and blue-purple **Indigo Aura** (also called **Tanzan Aura**). *(or-uh)*

AFFIRMATION
"I believe in magic"

Aventurine

LUCK • GROWTH • ABUNDANCE

⊛ **Color** Glittering green

⌖ **Born in** India, Brazil

♋ **Chakras** Solar Plexus, Heart

◊ **Water Cleansing** ☒ Y ☐ N

MAGIC Are you a lotto-ticket-buying, four-leaf-clover-seeking, lucky-horseshoe believer? Then Aventurine might be a perfect crystal for your! A popular lucky talisman since ancient days, Aventurine is one of the classic crystals of luck, prosperity, and overall good fortune. A form of microcrystalline Quartz embedded with shimmering green Fuchsite, Aventurine shares many of Fuchsite's magical qualities, especially its connection to nature and the elemental world of fairies and earth spirits. A prosperous harvest was one of the most precious things one could receive in the ancient world, which I'm guessing is where Aventurine's association with luck and abundance was born. Plants thrive around green Aventurine; place small pieces on the soil of your houseplants to give them some extra love, and try 'gridding' your garden by placing crystals in all four corners — the fairies and earth spirits of your land will be extra grateful. To manifest another kind of green abundance ($$$), try keeping Aventurine anywhere you keep cash, from wallets to cash registers to piggy banks.

NOTES Aventurine is a variety of Quartz with glittering mica inclusions. While green is its most common and best-known color, Aventurine comes in other shades, notably blue and reddish-brown. Occurring only in *massive* (non-crystallized) form, Aventurine is very affordable in a variety of polished shapes and raw pieces, and has often been used as an inexpensive alternative to Jade, another lucky crystal. **Aventurine Glass** (also known as **Goldstone**) is an artificial glass. *(ah-ven-chur-een)*

AFFIRMATION
"I am lucky"

Azurite

SERENITY • ILLUMINATION • STRESS RELIEF

⊛ **Color** Royal blue

⌬ **Born in** Mexico, Morocco, DRC

⟁ **Chakras** 3rd Eye, Throat

◊ **Water Cleansing** Polished pieces only

MAGIC Azurite is a special crystal of illumination and insight. Just having a piece of this royal-blue mineral in your presence helps melt old grudges, outdated beliefs, and limiting fears from both your psyche and aura. Azurite asks you to rise up and become your best self. It helps you remain calm and grounded as you work through your personal triggers and edges, guiding you towards true inner tranquility. A crystal of awareness expansion, place Azurite on your 3rd eye chakra *(between your eyebrows)* for a zap of clarity and serenity whenever overwhelm rears its stressful head: inhale deeply, and exhale a gray storm cloud of your worries, indecisions, and fears. Watch them gently float away over a royal-blue sea of Azurite awareness and clarity. *Gentle peace, deep serenity*. Azurite is also wonderful for clearing your energy after difficult conversations or emotional outbursts; simply hold a crystal to your throat or 3rd eye to help you recenter and rebalance.

NOTES Azurite occurs worldwide in more than 150 different crystal formations, from mossy-looking *druzy* crystals on rock *(pictured)*, to crystals with such intense saturation that their blue color can only be seen when held up to a light source. Often forms combined with green Malachite, which adds a heart-opening boost to Azurite's metaphysical gifts. **K2 Azurite** (also called **K2 Jasper** or **K2 Granite**) is a unique variety of Azurite dots encased in black and white granite. *(aah-zhur-rite)*

AFFIRMATION

"I allow serenity"

Bloodstone

MYSTICISM • PROTECTION • DETOX

✸ **Color** Dark green + red

⌖ **Born in** India, South Africa, Madagascar

♨ **Chakras** Root, Sacral, Heart

◊ **Water Cleansing** ☒ Y ☐ N

MAGIC *Middle Earth. Hogwarts. Westeros.* If you know and love at least one of these realms, mythical Bloodstone is most likely a magic-filled talisman for you. A stone of many legends, Bloodstone was known as *Martyr's Stone* in the Middle Ages, a favorite for Christian jewelry as it was believed to represent the red blood of Christ on green moss. But the magic of this mineral goes beyond its fabled past. Modern-day mystics prize Bloodstone for its protective and grounding gifts, as well as its ability to open portals to the elemental realm of elves, gnomes, and fairies. If you wish to awaken your inner magician, Bloodstone may hold an important key. It creates a protective aura around you, so tuck a piece into your pocket, bra, or bag on days when you need an extra-potent boost of courage and protection, aka when you need some Gandalf-Dumbledore wizardry on your side. And the magic doesn't end there: Bloodstone can also help strengthen your overall wellness due to its ability to clear toxins, making it a healing crystal ally for when you're cleansing, detoxing, or recovering from a night of magic-making.

NOTES Bloodstone is a variety of Jasper. Historically it was called **Heliotrope,** still occasionally used as an alternate name. Several African countries are current sources of affordable Bloodstone (often called **African Bloodstone**), which generally has more red than 'classic' Bloodstone, plus inclusions of gray Chalcedony. Bloodstone is a March birthstone.

AFFIRMATION
"I am surrounded by magic"

Brandberg Amethyst

SPIRITUAL AWAKENING • TRANSFORMATION • LIGHTWORKER MAGIC

✳ **Color** Purple, smoky, clear

◎ **Born in** Namibia

🪷 **Chakras** All

♡ **Care** Fades in direct sunlight

◌ **Water Cleansing** ☒ Y ☐ N

MAGIC Carefully extracted by hand from the fire-colored Brandberg mountain area, long revered as a sacred energy vortex, many crystal healers consider Brandbergs to be among the most powerful crystals on the planet. A Brandberg's unique magic comes from its ability to activate and harmonize all of your chakra centers, including recently identified 'modern' chakras. Essentially, a Brandberg plugs you into a giant energy upgrade, helping align your energy with the new consciousness that is arising on our planet right now. Smoky Brandbergs are considered by many to be the finest crystals for dissolving negative energies and replacing them with light; meditating or sleeping with this crystal can be deeply transformative. Does this all sound intense, maybe even a bit over your head? Don't worry! Brandbergs find their way to those who are in a moment of rapid spiritual evolution, and ready to handle strong magic. So if one of these special crystals finds its way to you, trust it. Your Brandberg is a wise and ancient friend who has shown up at the perfect time, to support you as you continue further in your soul's evolution.

NOTES Most commonly found as single crystal points, Brandbergs are often a fusion of three varieties of Quartz: Amethyst, Clear Quartz, and Smoky Quartz. Extra-special Brandbergs feature *enhydros,* bubbles of ancient water that visibly move when the crystal is rotated. Because they're so limited due to their small mining area, it's becoming common for crystals from other countries to be passed off as Brandbergs, so be sure to buy from a trusted source to ensure you're getting a true Brandberg. **Goboboseb Amethyst** is an alternate name. Amethyst is a February birthstone. *(brand-burg)*

AFFIRMATION
"I am transforming"

Calcite

HEALING • ANGELIC GUIDANCE • ENERGY AMPLIFIER

✳ **Color** All shades of the rainbow
◎ **Born in** Worldwide
❧ **Chakras** Varies according to color
♡ **Care** A softer mineral, use care
◊ **Water Cleansing** ☐ Y ☒ N

MAGIC *Be Your Own Healer.* Found worldwide in a beautiful rainbow of colors, Calcite's #1 gift is its ability to hold space for gentle healing of all types — physical, emotional, mental, spiritual. Unlike some other crystal varieties that shake things up, energetically speaking, Calcite works gently, asking *"What is ready to easily transform and evolve?"* Simply being in this mineral's presence helps us slow down, so we have more energetic space in which to rebalance and recharge. Keep whichever varieties feel the most aligned to your current healing needs in spaces where you spend the most time. Calcites are also the best crystals for *distance healing*, the gift of sending love and support to others from afar. To do this, sit in a quiet place while holding a piece of Calcite, and bring an image of your loved one into your mind. Imagine a golden light surrounding them, enveloping them in a glowing bubble. Don't project any specific outcomes or wishes; simply send love, bathing them in your care and support. Trust that whatever is for their highest good will manifest. This is a very 'energetically clean' way to support others, and is a beautiful healing gift to share.

NOTES A calcium carbonate, Calcite is one of the most abundant mineral families, and is found in virtually every country on earth. It crystallizes in a variety of shapes and colors, and ranges from affordable polished pieces to pricey crystallized clusters *(pictured: Optical Calcite).* Calcite often forms as little white or clear crystals on other minerals, adding a lovely boost of healing energy to the overall vibration of the host mineral. A softer mineral, Calcite cleaves and scratches easily, so use care. *(kal-site)*

AFFIRMATION
"I am healing"

1

2

3

4

CALCITE VARIETIES:

1) BLUE CALCITE Are you feeling overwhelmed, overstimulated, overextended? This powder-blue crystal calms everything down so your nervous system can gently start to re-regulate. Gentle is the keyword here; there are times when you need an energy booster shot, and times when you need a quiet energy cocoon. Blue Calcite is a crystal for the cocoon days. Carry a small piece with you as a protective buffer from the intensity of your day. *Chakras: Throat, Crown*

2) CARIBBEAN CALCITE Although this crystal originates far from the waters of the Caribbean — in the deserts of Pakistan — it's obvious why it has such a vacation-vibes name; stare into its beachy swirls and you'll instantly feel like you can relax a bit more. *Aaahh*. A mini vacation in a crystal. Refresh your daily vibration by keeping one within view wherever you tend to feel the most stress. One of the newest members of the Calcite family, it is also sold as **Blue Aragonite**. *Chakras: Throat, Crown*

3) COBALTO CALCITE Has love got you very down, or your confidence been badly shaken by a romance? Cobalto Calcite is here to turn that heart-frown upside down, sweetheart. This sparkly pink crystal wants to remind you that love can feel very fun, playful, and joyful. And not only *can* love feel like this, it *should* feel like this; you are so, so deserving of joyful, supportive love! Keep this bright crystal somewhere it will bring a smile. Some clusters include bright pops of green Malachite, for an extra boost of self-compassion and forgiveness. *Chakras: Heart, Root. (ko-ball-tow)*

4) GREEN CALCITE *What makes your soul-garden grow?* It is so important to make space for the small and easily overlooked things that add up to create a balanced, well-nurtured life. Green Calcite helps you make more time and space for the gentle joys of life: the slow walks, the nourishing bites, the sweet hugs, the soft quiet. Be a good gardener of your life, so that your life-garden can take the very best care of you. Alternative names: **Aqua / Pistachio / Seafoam Calcite**. *Chakras: Heart, Throat*

continues...

5) MANGANO CALCITE Sweet Mangano Calcite has the gentlest energy of the Calcite family. These cloud-pink crystals blend particularly well with *Reiki*, an ancient Japanese energy technique that activates the healing energy already present inside you. Place a crystal on your heart, or hold while curled up on your side, and imagine yourself surrounded by a glowing pink bubble. Allow yourself to rest, to be nurtured, to heal. This is a wonderful crystal to help children feel calmer. Also called **Pink Calcite**. *Chakra: Heart (<u>main</u>-guh-no)*

6) OPTICAL CALCITE Sometimes what you most need is a fresh perspective. Luckily for us, Optical Calcite is a magical tool for this. This crystal-clear mineral forms in perfect rhomboid shapes, rainbow-filled parallelograms that offer a fresh filter. Gaze through one to give your subconscious a powerful shift, or hold to your 3rd eye (*between your eyebrows)* when having a hard time making decisions. Let this crystal remind you that 'reality' is nothing more than an optical illusion; nothing is permanent, nothing is insurmountable, and nothing — absolutely nothing! — is impossible. Also called **Clear Calcite** or **Iceland Spar**. Rarer varieties are light yellow, pink, lavender. *Chakras: 3rd Eye, Crown*

7) ORANGE / YELLOW CALCITE Feeling run down, hungover, that-time-of-the-month-ish? Orange / Yellow Calcite is a healing balm for cramps, colds, hangovers, and upset stomachs. Place one on your belly, and relax as its gentle, warming energy spreads through you. Pair with a cup of honeyed tea to amplify its soothing magic. **Stellar Beam Calcite**, a variety that forms stunning points, helps you gently expand into being able to hold new levels of energy (also called **Dogtooth** /**Elmwood Calcite**). There are many alternative names for orange and yellow-colored Calcite, including **Amber / Citrine** / **Honey** / **Golden** / **Lemon Calcite**. *Chakras: Sacral, Solar Plexus*

8) RED CALCITE Do you prioritize other people's needs over your own? Are you so used to taking care of everyone else that if I asked, *"What do you need right now to feel better?"* you might not be able to crack through the overwhelm to even begin to feel into your answer? Red Calcite would be a supportive crystal for you, my overwhelmed and overgiving friend. It will gently help make some energetic space for your *own* nourishment, so you can refill your drained cup. This is a very supportive crystal for parents and caregivers. *Chakras: Root, Sacral*

5

6

7a

8

7b

Carnelian

ENERGY • VITALITY • FERTILITY

✳ **Color** Fiery orange + red
☄ **Born in** India, Brazil, Madagascar
🜄 **Chakras** Sacral, Root
💧 **Water Cleansing** ☒ Y ☐ N

MAGIC *Smoke alert*. Carnelian gets inner fires burning hot and bright! Fire-colored Carnelian's gifts lie in igniting energizing flames under you in a myriad of magical ways. **Q:** Are you lacking the energy and focus to bring your creative daydreams into reality? **A:** Carnelian. **Q:** Could your confidence as a vibrant, sexy creature use a major boost? **A:** Carnelian. **Q:** Do your bedroom activities need some new spice? **A:** Carnelian! This revitalizing gem is one of my go-to crystals for women struggling with infertility, and it makes a wonderful gift for people preparing for or healing from a major physical accomplishment (childbirth, surgery, marathon, etc). Carnelian is also extremely helpful for energizing more modest physical goals, like *finally* committing to that exercise routine you've been wanting to embody.

Bring Carnelian to the gym with you: it's a pocket-sized personal trainer who will energize you to do your very best! Prized by everyone from the ancient Romans to the emperor Napoleon for good reason, add some Carnelian magic into your life and get ready to shine extra, extra bright.

NOTES Carnelian is the orange-red variety of translucent Chalcedony. **Sard** is an alternative name for darker material. Specimens that show banding can also be called **Carnelian Agate** or **Sardonyx** (note: if you spend any time shopping for this crystal, you'll quickly notice that the lines dividing the varieties are loose). Occurring only in *massive* (non-crystallized) form, Carnelian has been polished for use as a semiprecious gemstone since antiquity. *(kar-nee-lee-yin)*

AFFIRMATION
"I am energized"

Celestite

ANGELIC GUIDANCE • INTUITION • SERENITY

✳ **Color** Translucent blue

◔ **Born in** Madagascar

♋ **Chakras** Throat, Crown, 3rd Eye

♡ **Care** Fades in direct sunlight

◊ **Water Cleansing** ☐ Y ☒ N

MAGIC *Calling all angels.* Heavenly-blue Celestite clusters are sparkling gifts of angelic intuition. This crystal connects you with a personal hotline to your angels, giving you direct access to guidance from the higher realms, and strengthening your trust in gut instincts, inspirations, and magical serendipities. Keep a cluster of this celestial crystal by your bedside, and you will be gifted with transformative messages and guidance during dreamtime. A cluster kept in your workspace will spark creative inspiration and intuitive breakthroughs. One of the most soothing and peace-filled crystals, Celestite is also magical at calming stress and anxiety. Are you one of those people who can't stop overthinking *everything*? Having Celestite around will help you transform perfectionist tendencies, and lighten up your self-limiting habits of worrying and overanalyzing (Virgos, this crystal is a must for you!). One of my personal favorites, Celestite's special brand of angelic magic is truly a gift sent from heaven.

NOTES The best-known variety of Celestite are geodes from the island of Madagascar. When broken open, the chalky geodes reveal sparkling masses of tabular, light blue crystals. This is a softer mineral, so handle with care as crystals can be easily damaged. Keep out of direct sun and charge only in moonlight. Polished, opaque 'Celestite' pieces are almost always blue Calcite misleadingly labeled. **Celestine** is this mineral's original name, and is the name used by mineralogists. *(sell-us-tite)*

AFFIRMATION
"I am divinely guided"

Chalcedony

SELF-CARE • STRESS RELIEF • CALM

✳ **Color** Translucent pastels

◎ **Born in** Brazil, India, Namibia

🪷 **Chakras** Throat, Heart, Crown

💧 **Water Cleansing** ☒ Y ☐ N

MAGIC *Cosmic Self-Care.* Pastel Chalcedony's energy is like a soothing lullaby encapsulated in a crystal. One of the most calming members of the crystal realm, these gently luminous gemstones help you intentionally commit time and space to care for yourself, channeling healing and inner radiance to replace stress and burnout. A powerful anti-inflammatory for both mind and spirit, hold a polished stone when you need a moment of peace. Gently run your fingers over its silky surface and *breathe*, imagining yourself surrounded by a luminous, pastel bubble of healing light. Chalcedony added to a bubble bath is my favorite way to soak in its nurturing energy. A piece under your pillow can banish nightmares and restless sleep. And it's very soothing for littles — put a Chalcedony crystal in their bedroom to help them sleep.

NOTES Chalcedony is a mineral family of translucent microcrystalline Quartz (Quartz with crystals too small to see with the human eye). Translucent-white in its pure state, inclusions transform Chalcedony into a wide variety of minerals, notably Agate, Jasper, and Onyx — yes, they are all varieties of Chalcedony! As there are many overlapping and non-precise names used for Chalcedony varieties it can get confusing. A simple breakdown: Chalcedony is *translucent* (light can shine through), Jasper is *opaque* (no light shines through), and Agate / Onyx have *bands of both*. In jewelry, Chalcedony usually refers to milky-blue gemstones. **Aqua Chalcedony** is usually glass, or artificially dyed. *(kal-seh-duh-nee)*

AFFIRMATION
"I nurture + love myself"

Charoite

COSMIC INTUITION • INNER STILLNESS • MEDITATION

✳ **Color** Iridescent violet swirls

🎯 **Born in** Russia

☸ **Chakras** 3rd Eye, Crown

💧 **Water Cleansing** ☒ Y ☐ N

MAGIC Charoite whispers of deep magic. Named after the Russian word for enchantment, this rare, violet-swirled mineral is only found in one of the coldest regions on the planet, a remote area of northern Siberia. Holding a resonance to the ancient frozen earth in which it was born, Charoite can facilitate profound depths of inner stillness and journeying. This is a powerful crystal for dropping into deep levels of psychic awareness and intuition, a 'crystal psychedelic' that can help you tap into unseen realms, both within and without (no trip to the jungle or illegal substances needed). Simply meditate with Charoite on your 3rd eye (*between your eyebrows*) to amplify your connection to your higher self and receive intuitive cosmic downloads. Or use it as a dreamtime tool: sleep with one

near you, and upon waking be sure to write down or voice-record your dreams before they fade. If you wish to see beyond the veil, unleash your inner mystic, and connect with the unseen world, give Charoite a try and see what cosmic doors it helps open for you.

NOTES Originally called **Lilac Stone**, Charoite was discovered in Siberia in the 1940s. Although unusually affordable relative to its rarity, fakes are still very common (both human-made resin and purple-dyed minerals); real Charoite has an iridescent sheen, delicate swirls that have a unique sense of movement, and commonly shows black and white areas, in addition to violet. (*char-oh-ite*)

AFFIRMATION
"I channel cosmic magic"

Chrysoberyl

CURIOSITY · AUTHENTICITY · PROTECTION

✳ **Color** Yellow, brown, green, purple-red
🎯 **Born in** Brazil, Sri Lanka, Madagascar
🐾 **Chakras** 3rd Eye, Solar Plexus
💧 **Water Cleansing** ☒ Y ☐ N

MAGIC *Embrace your Inner Explorer.*
Have you ever been made to feel like your natural curiosity is a nuisance, a bother, an imposition? Well, Chrysoberyl is here to remind you that your vibrant sense of curiosity is actually one of your biggest gifts, magic maker. You are a soul-explorer, bringing fresh insights and clarity to the planet — and that is something to be celebrated! This 3rd eye gemstone has been treasured for thousands of years as a healing and protective amulet, especially for eye and vision issues. Let it help you 'see' better, in both your inner and outer worlds. The best-known variety is **Alexandrite,** a color-changing birthstone for June babies. Alexandrite is one of the rarest gemstones in the world, however, so most of us will never have the chance to own a natural one.

But if lab-grown crystals 'feel' good to you, treat yourself to a sparkling lab-grown Alexandrite!* Keep exploring and asking those good questions, magic maker. Your curiosity is a superpower.

(Sidenote: the crystal community can get very judgy about lab-grown vs. natural-grown crystals. There's no need to get caught up in judgment; as with all things crystal-related, simply listen to your inner intuition, and do what feels right for you.)

NOTES Chrysoberyl is a rarer precious gemstone, so you're most likely to encounter it in fine jewelry, particularly antique jewelry. **Cat's Eye** is a rare variety that shows *chatoyancy,* a band of light that appears to move across the surface when viewed from different angles, resembling the eye of a cat. This effect is caused by the reflection of light off internal, needle-like inclusions. **Alexandrite,** the rarest form of Chrysoberyl, is a June birthstone. *(kris-uh-bear-ul)*

AFFIRMATION
"My curiosity is a superpower"

Chrysocolla

EMPOWERED FEMININE • GODDESS ENERGY • FERTILITY

Color Blue-green

Born in USA, Peru, Congo, Mexico

Chakras Throat, Heart

Water Cleansing Polished pieces only

MAGIC You know those women who make you feel nurtured, inspired — *alive* — just by being in their presence? Who illuminate an entire room with their inner glow? If you're drawn to embodying an empowered form of feminine energy — or you crave being surrounded by powerful, lit-up women — Chrysocolla is a potent crystal for you. Empowered femininity takes many forms and faces within our religions and myths: from Christianity's ultra-nurturing Mother Mary to Buddhism's Kuan Yin, gentle goddess of compassion; from Hinduism's take-no-BS Kali, fierce goddess of destruction to sensual Oshun, Yoruba goddess of love. Each of these holy women embody different aspects of the energy of the Divine Feminine, an elemental power every human can benefit from nurturing within themselves. Meditate with bright Chrysocolla resting on your throat or heart to empower your connection with this divine energy. Allow it to infuse you with intuitive wisdom, grace, and power (and if you're struggling with fertility issues, this is a healing crystal that can help you navigate through the challenges). Let the magic of Chrysocolla guide you on your journey towards becoming a more empowered, radiant, divine version of yourself.

NOTES Chrysocolla's color is created from oxidized copper. Often mistaken for Turquoise, this soft mineral is commonly found in deposits with Turquoise and other copper-based minerals such as green Malachite and blue Azurite. **Eilat Stone** is a beautiful blend of these copper-based minerals. Chrysocolla forms in a variety of shapes, from delicate velvety specimens to larger 'masses' that are polished into a variety of shapes. *(kris-oh-ko-la)*

AFFIRMATION

"I am empowered"

Chrysoprase

FRESH START • GROWTH • FORGIVENESS

✳ **Color** Mint to apple green

◉ **Born in** Australia, Brazil, Madagascar

❀ **Chakras** Heart, Solar Plexus

♡ **Care** May fade in sunlight

◊ **Water Cleansing** ☒ Y ☐ N

MAGIC This springtime-green gemstone buzzes with the energy of fresh starts and new beginnings. If you're hoping to manifest exciting new opportunities — or if you're in a period of transition and need support — Chrysoprase is a fantastic crystal for manifesting and supporting change. Simply keep one in your daily space (somewhere you'll see it regularly) and take a quick moment each time you see it to imagine yourself surrounded by a bright-green bubble of sparkling energy. This will only take a second, but trust me, it will infuse you with a fresh and transformative vibration every time. Chrysoprase is also a powerful stone of forgiveness. Because *you can't make room for the new if you're still holding onto the old*. So spend some time with your Chrysoprase near your heart to help you release, forgive, and transform. You can wear it in a necklace to keep its energy close to your heart, or meditate with a crystal on your heart chakra while repeating its affirmation. If you're ready to embrace new beginnings and let go of the past, Chrysoprase is a perfect crystal companion for this moment in your journey.

NOTES Chrysoprase is the name used for bright-green Chalcedony. One of the rarest and most valuable Chalcedony varieties, gem-quality Chrysoprase is generally vibrant and translucent, while inexpensive tumbled stones are opaque, and blended with inclusions. **Prase** is an alternate name for darker specimens. Although **Aquaprase** and **Lemon / Citron Chrysoprase** are not 'true' Chrysoprase, mineralogically speaking, they hold similar metaphysical magic. Note that dyed Chalcedony is often misleadingly sold as genuine Chrysoprase. (*kris-oh-praise*)

AFFIRMATION
"I let go to allow something better"

Citrine

POSITIVE ENERGY • MANIFESTATION • GOAL-SETTING

Color Transparent orange + yellow

Born in Brazil, DRC, Namibia

Chakras Solar Plexus, Sacral

Care Fades in direct sunlight

Water Cleansing ☒ Y ☐ N

MAGIC *Take your Vitamin C(itrine)!* Sunshine encapsulated in a crystal, sparkling Citrine powers up your core to help manifest your wildest dreams into reality, and raises your overall energy to a much sunnier vibration. Have a pile of goals, dreams, and to-do lists to conquer? Try the following Citrine meditation, useful for everyone from type-A super-achievers to daydreamers who struggle with follow-through. One of the most popular healing crystals for very good reason, sunshiny Citrine will spread joyful, energizing, and healing vibrations everywhere you keep it.

RITUAL To manifest a specific goal from your wishlist or to-do list, hold a piece of Citrine in your hands, and imagine the goal inside a clear balloon hanging a few feet in front of you. Picture flickering flames beginning to emerge from the crystal, moving towards the balloon, and slowly transforming it from clear to a golden-orange hue. When you're ready, give an imaginary puff and blow the balloon away, watching it float up, up and away, until you can't see it anymore. Take three deep breaths to anchor the energy in your body. *Manifesting magic!*

NOTES Citrine is the official name for Quartz with internal yellow or orange coloring. Almost all Citrine was originally Amethyst or Smoky Quartz, heated at high temperatures to change the internal color. Non-heated Citrine is rare, and typically a cloudy yellow-brown. While some prefer the name **Heated Amethyst** for treated specimens, this is technically redundant, both because Citrine is the accepted gemological name, and also because nearly all Citrine has been treated (including most sold as 'natural' — so if you wish to buy truly non-heated Citrine, buy from a trusted source). **Lemon Quartz** is an alternative name. Citrine is a November birthstone. (*sih-treen*)

AFFIRMATION

"I am a super-manifestor"

Clear Quartz

ENERGY TRANSFORMATION · HEALING · MANIFESTATION

✳ **Color** Crystal clear
⚙ **Born in** Worldwide
☁ **Chakras** All
◊ **Water Cleansing** ☒ Y ☐ N

MAGIC Revered as a powerful tool of transformative magic since time began, Clear Quartz lightens up, brightens up, and powers up our lives with its rainbow rays of magic. It's no exaggeration to say we live in a Quartz-powered world: clocks wouldn't work without the tiny crystals that keep them precisely ticking, and much of our essential technology relies on Quartz's electricity-conducting skills. But these crystals are so much more than just invaluable tools of technology! Clear Quartz is a master healer, energy transmitter, and connector to higher consciousness. A natural prism holding the full, sparkling spectrum of a rainbow, Clear Quartz is easily programmable as a personal magic tool: simply concentrate on your desired feeling or outcome while holding your crystal, and *voilà* — a tireless guide and cheerleader in crystal form. Clear Quartz also amplifies the healing magic of all other crystals. Follow your intuition when deciding how and where to use these powerful crystals, as they will clearly guide you. *Make your magic!*

NOTES Quartz is found all over the world, the most abundant crystal on our planet's surface. Composed of silicon dioxide, mineral inclusions transform Clear Quartz into many of the most popular crystal varieties, including Amethyst, Citrine, and Rose Quartz. Microcrystalline Quartz forms the basis of many other minerals, such as Agate, Chalcedony, and Jasper. Quartz crystals can be easily identified from other minerals by their six-sided crystal points.

AFFIRMATION
"I am magical"

Copper

GROUNDING • MANIFESTATION • ENERGY CONDUIT

✳ **Color** Metallic orange

☾ **Born in** USA, Peru, Chile

♨ **Chakras** Sacral, Solar Plexus, Heart

◌ **Water Cleansing** ☐ Y ☒ N

MAGIC Our Neolithic ancestors knew it, as did mystic ancient Egyptians: Copper is an amazing conduit for metaphysical and electrical energy alike. Copper has been utilized as an energy tool (both practical and magical) by humans for over 10,000 years. To connect yourself with its manifesting magic, meditate with a piece on your solar plexus chakra *(above your belly button)* when you need help manifesting your biggest, shiniest ideas. Copper will help bring them to life by 'grounding' them into current reality. Copper also makes a powerful travel buddy; I recommend bringing a small piece with you when you travel to help rebalance your energies after going a distance, and to ground into the energies of the place to which you've traveled (really helpful for jet lag!). In an ideal situation, hold Copper while your bare feet touch earth or grass; stay there for a few minutes to allow your energies to regulate and ground. If you can't easily access natural ground, get as close as you can to the earth (i.e. if you're in a tall hotel, do the above on the lowest floor you can access). **Rose Gold** is a blend of Copper and Gold that combines the magic of both into a beautiful, rosy metal. Rose Gold jewelry is my favorite suggestion for bringing Copper's grounding energy into your daily life.

NOTES Copper is a native element (*Cu*). It is estimated that our planet contains 5.8 trillion pounds, less than 12% of which has been mined in all of human history. Copper oxidizes green over time, and colors many green and blue minerals, including Turquoise, Malachite, Azurite, and Chrysocolla. Copper for crystal healing is usually sold as raw nuggets or small manufactured orbs.

AFFIRMATION
"I am grounded"

Danburite

HEART HEALING • NURTURING • REPARENTING

✳ **Color** Pale pink, clear, yellow

◉ **Born in** Mexico

❧ **Chakras** Heart, Crown

♡ **Care** Fades in direct sunlight

◊ **Water Cleansing** ☒ Y ☐ N

MAGIC Like a gentle embrace, Danburite wraps you in a cocoon of comforting, nurturing love. This is a wonderful crystal for when your day feels gray and you really, really need a hug. Remember those simple days of childhood when a hug from a parent could magically make everything okay? Heart-soothing Danburite holds a tender 'mothering' energy, but without any complicated history attached. And if you didn't have the experience of nurturing parenting, Danburite holds a safe space for you to heal your inner child, aka *reparent* yourself. This crystal is a powerful healing balm for those who have not received enough loving care, both in childhood and adulthood. When your heart feels sad, hold

a Danburite crystal to your chest, and take a deep breath. Danburite is also a wonderful crystal remedy if you have trouble sleeping, as it is deeply soothing to the nervous system. Place one on your bedside table, and this special crystal will join your heart and crown chakras to connect you with the angelic realm while you sleep, gently wafting you up to new heights of consciousness, serenity, and rest.

NOTES Danburite forms in unusual crystal 'blades' up to a foot in length, with tips crystallized in a wedge shape, similar to topaz crystals. It forms in translucent-to-transparent crystals colored clear, pink, and yellow. Pale pink crystals from Mexico are the most popular variety for crystal healing. Danburite crystal points chip easily, so use care. (*dan-burr-ite*)

AFFIRMATION

"I am so worthy of love + care"

Desert Rose

BALANCE • MEDITATION • GRIEVING

✳ **Color** Sandy brown
⌖ **Born in** Mexico, Morocco
⟡ **Chakras** Root, Crown, Sacral
◊ **Water Cleansing** ☐ Y ☒ N

MAGIC Formed from ancient desert sand, Desert Rose is the sandy cousin of Selenite (*page 229*), and holds many of the same cleansing properties, plus an added boost of grounding energy. Do you have a hard time sitting still or focusing? Desert Rose offers the gift of focused calm and balance, making this a great crystal for desks, workspaces, and anywhere you need access to clarity, focus, and concentration. One of my favorite crystals for meditation and yoga spaces, Desert Rose vibrates with a unique blend of root and crown chakra energies, creating a grounding + uplifting vibration that anyone near can tap into. It also supports processing grief, especially grief connected to death and pregnancy loss. Place this crystal on your low stomach to help you process, stabilize, and heal. I find Desert Rose's energy often resonates with men and boys, so if you're looking for a grounding gift for the special guys in your life, I highly recommend this crystal. Additionally, Desert Rose can be a great crystal buddy for children who struggle with hyperactivity, providing them with support and balance.

NOTES Desert Rose is a variety of the mineral gypsum, and is sold under several names, including **Sand Rose, Selenite Rose** and **Gypsum Rose**. Formed millions of years ago in water-saturated desert sand, its clusters of thin discs bear a resemblance to roses. Some specimens release a dusting of sand when touched and can erode easily, so handle with care.

AFFIRMATION
"I am balanced + grounded"

Diamond

COMMITMENT • INTEGRITY • FAITH

✳ **Color** Clear, yellow, smoky +

⌀ **Born in** Africa (various), Russia, Canada

🪷 **Chakras** Crown

💧 **Water Cleansing** ☒ Y ☐ N

MAGIC *You can do hard things.* Did you know that Diamonds form only under immense pressure? I'm talking *serious* pressure, equivalent to more than 50,000 times our atmosphere (!). And what does all that pressure create? One of the most unique things in nature, as Diamonds are the hardest substance created by the natural world. So it makes sense that these tough gemstones are paired with commitments as life-changing as marriage! The ancient Greeks even named Diamonds after the word for invincible, because that's exactly what this crystal offers us — help with keeping invincible, rock-solid commitments, both to ourselves and others. When you choose to wear a Diamond to honor a commitment, you are saying: *"I Commit. Like a Diamond, I will use whatever*

pressures come down the road to strengthen and transform this commitment into something even more radiant and valuable." Let Diamond help you stand strong in the face of anything, and be a reminder that there is always — *always* — light at the end of every tunnel, no matter how pressurized things get.

NOTES Diamonds are pure carbon. First valued in ancient India, their earliest source, they were used only in raw or cabochon form until the 1300s, when jewelers began faceting *(pictured: raw diamonds)*. They've been synonymous with engagement rings for less than 100 years, due to a massively successful marketing campaign in the 1930s. **Moissanite** and **Cubic Zirconia (CZ)** are popular lab-grown alternatives. Diamond is an April birthstone.

AFFIRMATION
"I am invincible"

137

Emerald

ABUNDANCE • RADIANT HEALTH • LUCK

⊛ **Color** Emerald green

◉ **Born in** Colombia, Brazil, Zambia

♨ **Chakras** Heart, Sacral

◊ **Water Cleansing** ☒ Y ☐ N

MAGIC Legendary beauties from Cleopatra to Elizabeth Taylor have famously prized these green jewels. They chose wisely: Emerald seriously amps up your personal magnetism and radiance, and can manifest huge gifts of magnetic good fortune, abundance, and health! A crystal of fertility and vitality, the ancient Egyptians used Emerald magic for everything from youthfulness and healthy childbirth, to protection in the afterlife. The Egyptians had the right idea; meditate with Emerald on your heart, or lower stomach *(sacral chakra)*, to tap into a vibration of vitality, fertility, and health. Add a crystal to your bathwater to infuse your entire body with its healing energies. And wear Emerald jewelry to surround yourself with its abundance vibration all day long.

Extremely protective, this is a great gemstone to take on the road with you as a talisman for safe travel. Emerald = helping you step into your true abundance, turn up the heat on your personal glow, and magnetize your very best life. *You are magnetic!*

NOTES Emerald is the green member of the beryl family. Although gemstone-quality Emeralds are pricey, Emeralds in tumbled stone form are inexpensive. Unlike gemstones, Emerald tumbled stones are generally opaque, with white and black inclusions. Emerald is a May birthstone.

AFFIRMATION
"I am magnetic"

Epidote

NATURE MAGIC • PSYCHIC INTUITION • WITCH WOUND

✳ **Color** Olive green

◎ **Born in** Peru, Pakistan, Mexico +

♋ **Chakras** 3rd Eye, Heart, Root

◌ **Water Cleansing** ☒ Y ☐ N

MAGIC *Witch. Witchcraft.* Potent words that have conjured fear and negativity for far too long. Put simply, most 'witches' center their lives around the natural world; the changing seasons, the ebb and flow of the moon, the patterns in the stars, and the potent healing power of plants, minerals, and animals. There's nothing scary or sinister about any of that, is there? It's time to transcend old and outdated misconceptions! If you're drawn to Epidote, it can mean that you're opening up to your inner psychic *knowing*, that sixth sense sometimes called serendipity or intuition — *your inner witchiness,* in other words. How exciting! Epidote is a potent crystal for healing *the witch wound,* a deep, intergenerational wounding many of us carry, born from the long history of persecution of those who worked with the energies of the natural world and intuitive healing. We are so blessed to be born in a time and place when we can explore 'woo-woo' interests (like crystals!) without fearing for our safety. We are so, so blessed. May our healing resonate backward to heal the wounds of those who came before us, and forward to illuminate the way for those who come after us.

NOTES 'Epidote' refers to both a family of minerals and the specific mineral Epidote, the most common member of that family. Often forming embedded in other minerals, tumbled Epidote stones are usually blended with white Quartz. *(ep-ih-doht)*

AFFIRMATION
"It is safe for me to be intuitive"

Fluorite

FOCUS • PRODUCTIVITY • CREATIVITY

✳ **Color** Green, purple, white +

◎ **Born in** Mexico, China

☋ **Chakras** Varies according to color

♡ **Care** Fades in direct sunlight

◊ **Water Cleansing** ☒ Y ☐ N

MAGIC *Unlock your inner genius.* Bestowed with the nickname 'Genius Stone' by medieval alchemists, Rainbow Fluorite is a crystal of focus, clear-thinking, and inspiration. If you find yourself struggling with concentration or hyperactivity, this multicolored gemstone can help clear mental fog and disorganization, making it an incredible ally for study, work, and overall productivity. Fluorite is very happy living on your desk, or in your general workspace. It's a 'cooling' crystal — soak in a bath with tumbled stones to reduce bodily pain, tensions, and infections. And carry a piece with you to stay focused and cool-headed during the hustle and bustle of daily life. Fluorite's chakra resonance changes according to the dominant color: green

and blue crystals help you express yourself clearly and concisely; purple crystals are aligned with the crown chakra and channel inspiration; pink crystals help calm overactive emotions; yellow crystals help you feel more confident. Cherished for centuries for its ability to enhance mental clarity and spark fresh inspiration, bring some Fluorite magic into your life and get ready to dazzle the world with your inner genius!

NOTES Fluorite spans the largest color range in the mineral kingdom, from colorless to a variety of bright shades. It most commonly crystallizes in geometric cubes. **Rainbow Fluorite**, the most popular variety *(pictured)*, has beautiful bands of color, and is sold in a wide variety of shapes and sizes. Green, purple, and white are the most common colors of Fluorite; pink and yellow are rare. *(flor-rite)*

AFFIRMATION
"I am a clear channel for magic"

Fuchsite

HOLISTIC HEALTH • HERBALISM • GREEN THUMB

✳ **Color** Shimmering green
◉ **Born in** Brazil
🐾 **Chakras** Heart
♡ **Care** Fades in direct sunlight
💧 **Water Cleansing** ☐ Y ☒ N

MAGIC A gentle heart-chakra crystal connected to the elemental realm of fairies, nature angels, and earth spirits, shimmery green Fuchsite helps channel healing magic from those realms, especially insights related to plants, herbal remedies, and holistic healing. If you have health issues you wish to treat holistically, this is a wonderful crystal to keep close while you research natural remedies, as it will help you zone in on what is best for *your* unique health and wellbeing. When you feel overwhelmed with information and in need of clarity, hold Fuchsite to your heart, inhale deeply through your nose, and exhale through your mouth with energy, like you're blowing cobwebs off something in front of you. This will help open space in the overwhelm for healing insight to come through. *Listen to your gut*. Fuchsite is also a great addition to your crystal collection if you wish to grow your green thumb, and makes a perfect gift for the plant-lovers in your life. Don't place this crystal directly on soil as it is damaged by water and sun; place it instead beside your houseplants. **Ruby Fuchsite**, a variety embedded with crimson Rubies, is a beautiful alternative with similar energies *(see page 223)*.

NOTES Fuchsite's distinctive sparkle comes from being a variety of mica, a spangled mineral that creates the shimmer in many cosmetics. Fuchsite is most commonly sold in small, raw pieces that leave a fun sparkle on whatever they touch. Also called **Green Muscovite**. **Verdite** is a variety with inclusions. Although often pronounced similarly to 'fuchsia,' the correct pronunciation is *fook-site.*

AFFIRMATION
"I am healing + growing"

Galena

FOCUS • PRODUCTIVITY • DISCIPLINE

✳ **Color** Metallic gray

◎ **Born in** Morocco, Bulgaria, Peru, USA

🪷 **Chakras** 3rd Eye, Root

♡ **Care** Lead-based, wash hands

○ **Water Cleansing** ☐ Y ☒ N

MAGIC Do you find that your attention starts going in a million directions right when you need to get some solid work done? Or maybe you pick up your phone a billion-trillion times a day as a distraction? It sounds like you might benefit from a little Galena magic in your workspace, friend. This geometric crystal is brilliant at helping calm overactive and distracted minds, and helps you ground into a vibration of focus for long-thought, in-depth productivity. A sister crystal to golden Pyrite, Galena helps you get down to the nitty-gritty details, while Pyrite is all about big-picture thinking and manifesting. These metallic minerals make a great workspace pair; keep them within eyesight while you're working, and whenever you feel your focus slipping (when you're tempted to pick up your phone for pure distraction, for example), instead take a moment to focus on these crystals' glittering, magnificently precise angles. Inhale / exhale a deep breath, give your head and hands a shake to release stuck energy, and then dive back into your work with refreshed focus and grit. The world needs your magnificent creations, so grab some Galena and get back to it, magic maker!

NOTES Galena crystallizes in cubic shapes, and often forms paired with a wide variety of minerals. It is mined mainly for industrial use as the primary ore of lead, though one of its oldest recorded uses is as kohl eyeliner, still used as traditional makeup in North Africa and the Middle East. Wash hands after touching and keep out of reach of little mouths due to Galena's lead content. (*guh-lee-na*)

AFFIRMATION
"My focus manifests magic"

Almandine Garnet

GROUNDING • PASSION • FERTILITY

�֎ **Color** Dark red

⌖ **Born in** India, China, Sri Lanka

⚘ **Chakras** Root, Sacral

◌ **Water Cleansing** ☒ Y ☐ N

MAGIC If you wish to explore uncharted territories and tap into your deepest passions, you need a solid foundation to fall back on. And that foundation, my friend, is a safe space. But what exactly does that mean? It means having access to an energy that makes you feel comfortable and secure, so you can take risks without fear. Enter Almandine Garnet. This dark red gemstone — the most popular and abundant Garnet variety — is such a supportive partner for this adventure called life, as it keeps you grounded, helps you establish boundaries, and can remove fear-based inhibitions that are holding you back. In short, this crystal can be a gamechanger for exploring beyond your comfort zone. Almandine Garnet is a crystal to keep close on days when you need extra support, whether that means tucking one into your pocket or bag, or wearing Garnet jewelry. This crystal is also all about generating passion: passionate creativity, passionate sensuality, *passionate living*. Potent fertility talismans, Almandine Garnet can seriously juice up your love life — try tucking one under your mattress to add spice to bedroom activities!

NOTES Garnets are a group of minerals that occur worldwide in a variety of colors and transparencies. When Garnet is used as a standalone name in jewelry, it typically refers to the Almandine variety. Although commonly sold as tumbled stones, Almandine Garnet naturally forms as faceted crystals worth searching out for their unique beauty. **Almandite Garnet** is an alternative name. Garnet is a January birthstone. *(all-mun-deen gar-net)*

AFFIRMATION
"It is safe for me to feel passion in my body + spirit"

GARNET VARIETIES:

1) DEMANTOID Demantoid means 'diamond-like' in Dutch, bestowed on this rare green variety due to its brilliant sparkle. Ultra refreshing and energizing! *Chakras: Solar Plexus, 3rd Eye, Heart. (duh-man-toyd)*

2) GROSSULAR This variety forms in a wide range of colors. The opaque green variety is often confused with Jade (or sold as Jade by less-than-honest dealers). A luck crystal, it helps increase your abundance in a grounded, sustainable way. Also called **African Jade**. *Chakras: Heart, Solar Plexus. (grah-syoo-lur)*

3) HESSONITE Popularly called **Cinnamon Stone** due both to its warm color and origin in the spicelands of Sri Lanka. Comforting and nurturing, this is a health tonic crystal, wonderful for infusing yourself with an overall sense of warm wellbeing. *Chakras: Sacral, Root. (heh-suh-nite)*

4) PYROPE This dark-red variety was popular with the ancient Greeks and Romans, and also abundantly used in Victorian jewelry. It's now in short supply, so you'll most likely encounter it in antique jewelry. Holds a similar energy to Almandine Garnet (see previous page). Also called **Bohemian Garnet**. *Chakras: Root, Sacral. (pie-rope)*

5) RHODOLITE A juicy, purple-red variety. Rhodolite is a blend of two garnet varieties — Pyrope and Almandine — and holds similar metaphysical energies to Almandine Garnet (see previous page). *Chakras: Root, Sacral. (row-doh-lite)*

6) SPESSARTINE A bright orange variety that often forms on Smoky Quartz. Supercharges fertility on all levels: from pregnancy and virility, to the inspiration for your next creative masterpiece. Also called **Spessartite**. **Mandarin Garnet** is a name used for extra-vivid gemstones. *Chakras: Sacral, Root. (spes-er-teen)*

7) TSAVORITE Discovered in the 1960s in Kenya's Tsavo National Park, this rare, springtime-green variety helps you confidently walk your own path. Keeps your intuition clear and unclouded by opinions and judgements from other people. *You do you*. Also called **Tsavolite**. *Chakras: Solar Plexus, 3rd Eye, Heart. (tsa-vuh-rite)*

8) UVAROVITE This rare, emerald-green variety is mostly available as moss-like crystals on a rock matrix. Helps heal scarcity wounds by strengthening your awareness that you are nourished and provided for by the web of life — always! *Chakras: Root, Heart. (oo-var-uh-vite)*

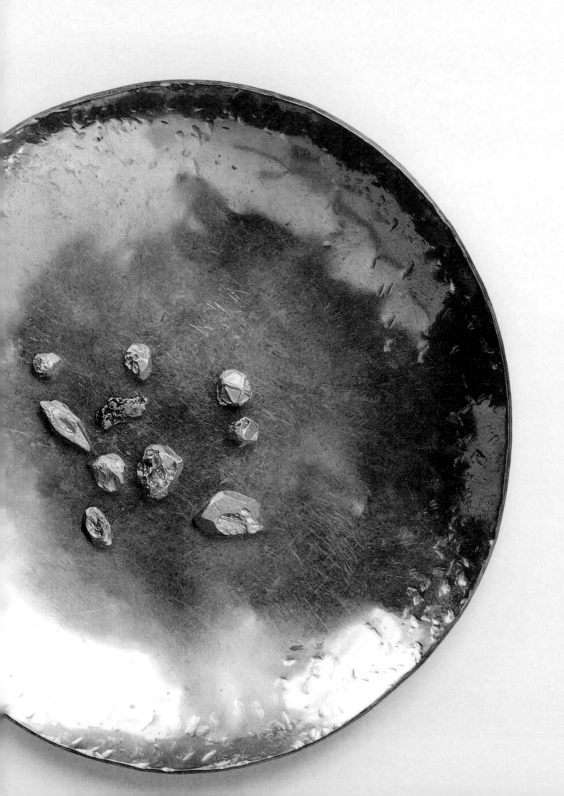

Gold

POWER • FREE WILL • MANIFESTATION

✳ **Color** Metallic-gold
⚲ **Born in** Worldwide
♋ **Chakras** All
◊ **Water Cleansing** ☒ Y ☐ N

MAGIC Oh, Gold... precious metal of endless legends, adventures, conquerings, exploitations, and so, so, *so* much desire. Thought to be formed by the energy of exploding stars (!), Gold's presence in our planet is still a mystery. Did it come from gold-infused stardust that sank into our planet's core after the Big Bang? Or did it embed itself through asteroid impacts billions of years ago? One thing that isn't a mystery, however, is just how much we humans love this shiny metal. The core of our planet swirls with molten Gold, and my hunch is that wearing it helps us plug into Earth's core vibration, which is one reason we crave it so strongly — it makes us feel more grounded and 'at home.' Gold also activates our connection to power and personal autonomy — aka our free will —

which is why it has been so entwined with the energy of power since our human story began. Gold asks each of us, *"How do you choose to show up in this world? Are you making choices from your highest self, or do you allow yourself to be guided by less-than-bright forces?"* And as we live in a universe of free will, Gold doesn't make the choice for you — it simply magnifies that which you choose. So choose well and wisely, magic maker. Do your best to live according to the oh-so-perfectly-named Golden Rule, so you give your Gold the very best of intentions and vibrations to magnify: *Do unto others as you would have them do unto you.*

NOTES Pure Gold is an element (*Au*). It is found as veins embedded in Quartz, as well as nuggets, crystals and tiny grains *(pictured: raw crystals and nuggets)*.

AFFIRMATION
"I am limitless"

Golden Healer Quartz

CONSCIOUSNESS EXPANSION • RADIANCE • FLOW

✳ **Color** Translucent yellow

⌖ **Born in** Arkansas (USA), Brazil

♨ **Chakras** All

♡ **Care** Fades in direct sunlight

◊ **Water Cleansing** ☐ Y ☒ N

MAGIC Golden Healer is an extremely high-vibration form of Quartz treasured by many crystal healers. It's considered to vibrate with *Christ Consciousness*, a term used in some spiritual traditions that refers not to Jesus specifically, but to a supremely elevated vibration of love. Esoteric stuff, I know! Don't overthink it; actually, try not to do any 'thinking' when working with Golden Healer, because this crystal's primary gift is taking you out of your human mind, and giving your consciousness space to expand. I'll let Golden Healer take the mic:

*"You are waking up. You are here in such an incredible moment of unprecedented potential and possibility. I know the news can often feel overwhelmingly doom and gloom, but you are here to **Radiate On A Higher Level**. Stay radiant. 'Reality' is a grand illusion. Don't self-limit! You are a magical being of free will and unlimited potential. Play, flow, explore, and connect with your Golden Potential. Trust that you are here to be in joy, and to be radiant."*

I couldn't have said it better myself.

NOTES Golden Healers are the yellow members of the Hematite Quartz family (to learn more about this crystal family, see page 158). They are translucent Quartz with a yellow coating (or internal inclusion) of iron-based Hematite and / or Goethite. The most beautiful crystals are primarily found in Arkansas or Brazil. **Solaris Quartz** are rare Golden Healers with rainbow iridescence *(pictured)*.

AFFIRMATION
"I let the light in"

Halite

HEART HEALING • ENERGY DETOX • BOUNDARIES

⊛ **Color** Light pink, white

⊘ **Born in** California

⬡ **Chakras** Heart

♡ **Care** Very fragile

◊ **Water Cleansing** ☐ Y ☒ N

MAGIC *Protect your heart.* A salt crystal, Halite is a powerful purifier of energies and environments. Formed from the salt of evaporated ancient seas, its delicate pink color is caused by tiny sea creatures; take a whiff and smell for yourself, this crystal smells like the sea! Salty Halite works hard to help 'evaporate' heartbreak and sadness in your heartspace, and helps you create stronger boundaries around your heart and emotions. Do you have a hunch that the relationship you're in isn't so healthy? Do some of your friends or family always leave you feeling more drained than supported? Are you an emotional empath, aka are you affected emotionally by other people's 'stuff' in a way that destabilizes you? Halite will help you separate from toxic or non-nourishing situations, by disconnecting you from people and energies that aren't serving you. *Clear out whomever and whatever is bringing you down, so you and your beautiful heart can soar.* This is a rarer crystal, so if you are unable to find one you can use Selenite and Rose Quartz together to create a similar vibration.

NOTES Halite is a sodium mineral better known as rock salt, mined worldwide for a huge variety of industrial purposes, including melting icy winter roads. Cubic crystal clusters are rare, as they are very delicate. Pink Halite primarily comes from an ancient lakebed in the Mojave Desert, Southern California. Halite is a fragile mineral that 'melts' in humid environments (so be sure to keep clusters very dry), and fades in direct sunlight. *(hal-ite or hay-lite)*

AFFIRMATION

"I am clearing out whomever + whatever dims my heart-light"

Hematite

RECHARGING • REBALANCING • GROUNDING

✳ **Color** Metallic dark gray
◎ **Born in** Brazil, USA, China, Morocco
✿ **Chakras** Root
◊ **Water Cleansing** Polished pieces only

MAGIC *Recharge yourself.* Do you get lost in unproductive worrying or reminiscing? Hematite helps anchor you in the present moment, making it a very helpful crystal for those who tend to get stuck in the past or future. We are each encased in our own personal magnetic sphere, similar to the magnetic field encompassing our planet. Hematite, an iron-based mineral with magnetic properties, is a powerful crystal tool for recharging your personal wiring and energy grid when life's stressors bring you close to short-circuiting. Slip a stone into your pocket to recharge and rebalance during your daily activities, or tuck one into your chair for continuous grounding during your workday. At the end of a long day, add a polished Hematite to your bath (by your feet) to help you release the day's stress. It also makes a great travel buddy, due to its protective and anti-jet-lag vibes. Hematite can also help mine down into issues buried deep in your emotional psyche, history, and ancestral lineage (*similarly to Hematite Quartz — see next page*). This crystal doesn't mess around, so if Hematite feels too intense (you'll know — it just won't feel right), try Black Tourmaline, Smoky Quartz or Hematite Quartz instead, as their energies tend to be gentler.

NOTES Hematite (also spelled Haematite) is a dense iron ore; its heaviness is a helpful identifying feature. It crystallizes in a diverse range of forms, including bubbly-looking *botryoidal* clusters, and is most commonly available as polished pieces. Water will rust raw specimens. **Magnetic Hematite** is human-made. (*hem*-uh-tite or *heem*-uh-tite)

AFFIRMATION
"I am recharged"

Hematite Quartz

ANCESTRAL HEALING • STRENGTH • FERTILITY

⊛ **Color** Shades of red

⌖ **Born in** Worldwide

☙ **Chakras** Root, Sacral, Heart

◊ **Water Cleansing** ☒ Y ☐ N

MAGIC For starters, let's clarify something that gets confusing. Reddish minerals that are a combination of Quartz and Hematite are sold under many names, including **Agnitite**, **Harlequin Quartz**, **Hematite Quartz**, **Hematoid Quartz**, **Fire Quartz**, **Ferruginous Quartz**, **Pink Amethyst**, **Pink Lemurian Quartz**, **Red Quartz**, **Red Healer Quartz**, and **Strawberry Quartz**. Although each variety looks a bit different, they are essentially the same mineral — Quartz + Hematite — and their main healing gifts are similar. These crystals are strengthening, energizing, purifying little powerhouses. The iron in Hematite resonates with the iron that runs red through our veins, making these crystals a wonderful tonic for fatigue and low energy, both physical and spiritual. Carry one with you throughout your day,

and tuck one under your mattress or pillow for nighttime healing. Hematite Quartz helps facilitate deep healing of things you've inherited through your bloodline; the ancestral grief and trauma of ancestors who came before you. *Heal now for all of them.* Place a crystal on your body wherever you feel led, and allow yourself to feel and release emotions as they arise. Let energies move through and out; don't be afraid to move your body or make sounds. If you feel the need for extra support, place grounding crystals like Smoky Quartz or Black Tourmaline touching the soles of your feet.

NOTES Quartz with an inclusion, coating, or staining of iron-based Hematite is found worldwide and sold under many names. **Lepidocrocite** *(bottom crystal pictured)* is Quartz combined with iron-based Goethite, and holds similar energies to Hematite Quartz. *(hem-uh-tite or heem-uh-tite)*

AFFIRMATION
"I honor + purify my connection with my ancestors"

Herkimer Diamond

HIGH VIBRATION • SOUL PURPOSE • ENERGY UPGRADE

✷ **Color** Clear to lightly smoky

◎ **Born in** New York (USA)

⬡ **Chakras** Crown, 3rd Eye

⬠ **Water Cleansing** ☒ Y ☐ N

MAGIC *Lightworker upgrade.* A Lightworker is someone devoted to following what lights up their soul, and therefore lights up the world through their presence (if you're reading this book, you're very likely one!). To strengthen your connection to Source Energy and brighten your light, add a glittering Herkimer Diamond to your crystal toolkit for energetic support of the highest vibration. These double-terminated crystals can receive, transform, and release energy all at the same time, which make Herkimers one of the best crystals for giving yourself powerful energy 'tune-ups.' Simply place one on your body anywhere that feels energetically stuck or stagnant, breathe calmly and deeply, and let your Herkimer work its magic — it will help raise your vibration to the highest level currently possible. To infuse your entire aura with fresh energy, meditate with one on your 3rd eye (*between your eyebrows*), or touching the top of your head. Your inner sparkle will feel so refreshed and radiant! Wearing Herkimer Diamond jewelry is a beautiful way to keep this crystal's support flowing as you go about sharing your daily Lightworker magic.

NOTES Herkimer Diamonds are named after Herkimer County in Central New York, where they were discovered in the 1700s. These glassy quartz crystals often contain specks of black anthraxolite (ancient plant matter), and multiple crystals often form intertwined in stunning clusters. Similar double-terminated Quartz crystals from other locales are often sold as **Diamond Quartz** — I find their metaphysical energies to be equally magical. (*hurk-ih-mur*)

AFFIRMATION

"I am a Lightworker"

161

Pink Himalayan Samadhi Quartz

UNIVERSAL LOVE • PEACE • BLISS

⊛ **Color** Translucent pink

⚉ **Born in** India, Nepal

☸ **Chakras** Heart

♡ **Care** Fades in direct sunlight

◌ **Water Cleansing** ☒ Y ☐ N

MAGIC In Yoga, *samadhi* is a blissful state in which individual and universal consciousness unite. These blush-pink crystals, born in the homeland of Yoga, vibrate with a similar energy: Universal Love. When we talk about 'following guidance from our higher self,' what we mean is tapping into our innate knowledge of the highest and best action to take, aka allowing ourselves to be guided by Universal Love. To strengthen your connection to this transformative energy, do the following **Pink Light Meditation** with your Samadhi Quartz as often as you feel guided.

RITUAL Sit in a comfortable position and hold your crystal in your lap. Begin to breathe deeply. Visualize a sparkling beam of pink light emanating from your crystal,

and another beam flowing from your heart. As you continue to breathe deeply, see the two beams of light merge into one, growing stronger and more vibrant. Visualize this powerful beam of light rising up and flowing out of the room you're in, extending higher and higher until it reaches outer space. Watch as the light spreads out and envelops the entire planet in a shimmering, luminous bubble of healing energy. Stay here for a bit. *You are in the bubble, too.* When ready, gently pull the beam of light back down into your heart and crystal, and close with three deep, grateful breaths. Thank you for sharing this healing gift with all of us. *(Note: as these are rare crystals, you can substitute any pink crystal for this ritual).*

NOTES Himalayan Samadhi Quartz is a metaphysical name for rare, pink-colored quartz from the Himalayas. Colored by trace amounts of aluminum, phosphate, and hematite, most crystals are a light peachy-pink. Green chlorite inclusions are not uncommon *(see Lodolite, page 189).* *(suh-ma-dee)*

AFFIRMATION
"I hold the vibration of Love"

Howlite

POWER DOWN • CALMING • GROUNDING

✳ **Color** Opaque-white with gray veining
🌿 **Born in** Zimbabwe, USA, Canada
🪷 **Chakras** All
💧 **Water Cleansing** ☐ Y ☒ N

MAGIC *Power down your system*. Howlite works differently than many crystals. While the majority 'activate' your chakras (aka your personal energy system), Howlite has the opposite effect. It works similarly to a weighted blanket, or a white noise machine — placing this stone on a chakra helps dampen excessively buzzy energy, leading to a calmer state of being and lessened anxiety. Use your intuition to know where on your body to place Howlite, as every chakra center has times when it can benefit from a little 'quieting down.' For instance: overthinking? Place Howlite between your eyebrows (*3rd eye chakra*). Oversharing? Place Howlite on your throat (*throat chakra*). Overly sensitive? Place Howlite on the middle of your chest (*heart chakra)*. Have a bad case of comparison-itis? Place Howlite on your belly button *(solar plexus chakra)*. Overly horny? Place Howlite on your low stomach (*sacral chakra*). Carry this calming crystal with you on days when you need help being a little less reactive to the world around you, and tuck it under your pillow on nights when you struggle with insomnia.

NOTES Most Howlite sold today is actually **Magnesite**, a similar-looking mineral, however Howlite has become the common name used for both minerals in the crystal healing and jewelry world. Because its veining can look similar to the veining in Turquoise, Howlite is sometimes sold under the names **White Turquoise**, **White Buffalo Turquoise** or **White Buffalo Stone**. Blue-dyed Howlite is commonly sold as imitation Turquoise, sometimes called **Howlite Turquoise** or **Turquenite**. (*how-lite*)

AFFIRMATION
"I allow myself to power down + reset"

Iolite

CLARITY • SOUL PURPOSE • CALMS ANXIETY

✳ **Color** Violet-blue

◎ **Born in** India, Brazil, Sri Lanka

👁 **Chakras** 3rd Eye, Crown

💧 **Water Cleansing** ☒ Y ☐ N

MAGIC *Inner Vision.* This violet-blue crystal is magical at helping connect you with your inner WHY: *"Why do I stay stuck in this thought pattern? Why do I have these doubts and fears? Why am I interested in that person / that opportunity / that life change?"* Getting very clear and honest on your inner why is absolutely vital for cutting through confusion, and this crystal will help to either reaffirm where you are, or empower you to make a change. To connect with Iolite's gifts, place a crystal between your eyebrows *(3rd eye chakra)* while you ask yourself the questions to which you're seeking clarity. Wear this beautiful blue gemstone in jewelry to maintain a strong connection to your inner soul-compass as you go through your day. A calming crystal, Iolite is also very helpful for quieting insomnia and anxiety.

NOTES Named after the Greek word for violet, *ios*, Iolite is the gemstone form of the mineral cordierite. Translucent to transparent, it sometimes shows sparkling inclusions, called **Iolite Sunstone** or **Bloodshot Iolite**. Iolite is *pleochroic*, meaning it can exhibit different colors when viewed from different directions: blues, violets, grays, and even yellows. Unlike most blue gemstones, Iolite is generally not heat-treated to enhance its color. Also known as **Water Sapphire** and **Dichroite**. *(eye-oh-lite)*

AFFIRMATION
"I listen to my inner truth"

Jade

LUCK · SUCCESS · PROSPERITY

✳ **Color** Shades of green

◎ **Born in** Myanmar, Guatemala, China +

🪷 **Chakras** Solar Plexus, Heart

💧 **Water Cleansing** ☒ Y ☐ N

MAGIC Jade is a renowned crystal of prosperity and success, prized as a lucky talisman by everyone from the ancient Aztecs to modern tech moguls. The smooth green stones we call Jade are actually two different minerals, Jadeite and Nephrite, with two very different histories. The name Jade comes from the Spanish *piedra de ijada*, meaning 'stone of the side,' the name given by conquistadors to the green Jadeite they saw native Aztecs and Mayans using to cure internal pain. On the other side of the globe, Nephrite has been treasured in Chinese culture for thousands of years as a stone of spiritual purity and intellectual clarity. And for modern crystal lovers around the world, Jade is a classic choice for abundance and good fortune. Jade is a valuable crystal for *getting to know yourself*, an important

factor behind it having such a legacy as a crystal of luck and success. Because when you truly know yourself — when you get really clear and honest about *who* you are and *why* you came here — you can't help but focus your time and energy on things that are in natural alignment with your gifts and skills. Which leads to (you guessed it) success and 'luck' in the material world, as well as a deep, fulfilling sense of nourishing prosperity. *Be yourself*.

NOTES Both Jadeite and Nephrite occur in many different colors, green being the best known. Emerald-green Jadeite, known as **Imperial Jade**, is the most valuable variety, and one of the priciest gemstones in the world. Lavender-colored Jadeite is also highly prized. Note that a wide variety of green minerals (particularly Serpentine) are sold as inexpensive varieties of 'Jade.'

AFFIRMATION
"Being my true self manifests limitless abundance"

Jasper

GROUNDING • STABILIZING • STRENGTHENING

✳ **Color** All shades of the rainbow

◉ **Born in** Worldwide

❧ **Chakras** Root + varies by color

◊ **Water Cleansing** ☒ Y ☐ N

MAGIC Found on every continent, in every color, Jaspers are the opaque members of the Chalcedony family — which means that when you hold a Jasper up to light, no light passes through. These solid, no-drama gemstones are supremely grounding and stabilizing, and their primary gift is helping you feel stronger in both your physical and emotional bodies. Have you ever experienced a strong sensation of *siiiinking* into the ground, or the seat you're sitting in (perhaps when you've used certain substances)? That's the energy of these crystals; they ground you into the earth's energy. All Jaspers have root chakra energy as their base, with aspects of other chakras according to their color. A chakra layout using only Jaspers is like a visit to the chiropractor, extremely stabilizing and aligning; follow the *Complete Chakra*

Recharge instructions on page 55 to treat yourself to the experience. Jaspers are also the best crystals for *earthing*, the health practice of grounding into the earth's energy. Earthing is a very healing ritual for times when you feel anxious or spacy, and a must after traveling to connect yourself with the energy of your new location: hold a Jasper while you sit or stand outside (with your bare feet touching the ground) for a healing zap of Vitamin G, aka grounding. Turn the page to learn about popular varieties of this grounding mineral.

NOTES Jasper is the opaque variety of Chalcedony, which is a form of microcrystalline Quartz. Found worldwide in *massive* (non-crystallized) form, Jasper is broken down and polished into a wide variety of shapes. The name Jasper is applied to many opaque minerals that aren't 'true' Jasper, as they aren't varieties of Chalcedony; however, Jasper's metaphysical properties still apply.

AFFIRMATION

"I am supported by the earth's energy"

JASPER VARIETIES:

1) BUMBLEBEE JASPER* Holds an energizing, buzzy energy. A great crystal buddy for creative adventures and socializing.

2) DALMATIAN JASPER* Encourages loyalty and honesty. Anxiety-relieving and comforting.

3) DRAGON'S BLOOD JASPER* A blend of green Fuchsite and red Jasper. Protective, holds a similar energy to Bloodstone (see page 108).

4) K2 JASPER* Blue Azurite orbs in Granite. Holds a similar energy to Azurite (see page 107).

5) KAMBABA JASPER* Fossilized ancient algae. Helps you 'root down' to connect with healing earth energies.

6) LEOPARDSKIN JASPER* A spotted variety of many colors. Helps you hold healthy boundaries. Very protective.

7) MOOKAITE JASPER* Helps you have the confidence to express yourself. Don't be afraid to act large and in charge!

8) OCEAN JASPER A variety with delicate, multicolored dots and swirls. Reminds you to prioritize rest and rejuvenation, and gracefully go-with-the-flow.

9) PICASSO JASPER* Helps you find your creative happy place, and artistic focus. Forms in many colors, identifiable by thin, web-like lines. Also called **Spiderweb Jasper**.

10) PICTURE JASPER Quiets overactive mind-chatter, so you can see the bigger picture. Stabilizing for when you're overwhelmed. Helpful for meditation.

11) POLYCHROME JASPER (also called **Desert Jasper**) An earthy blend of all chakra colors from the heart down, this is a deeply calming variety.

12) RAINFOREST JASPER* Holds similar magic to Kambaba Jasper (see above). Also called **Rhyolite**.

13) RED JASPER The OG Jasper variety, treasured since antiquity for its health-giving, protective magic. Activates and protects your root chakra so you feel supremely safe, supported, ALIVE!!!

14) YELLOW JASPER Gets other people's 'issues' out of your psychic space, so you can be your true self. Helps release energies you have taken on that aren't yours to deal with. Energizing and stabilizing.

15) ZEBRA JASPER Protective, helps you feel safe on your day-to-day adventures.

Although popularly known as a Jasper variety, mineralogically this is not true Jasper.

Jet

BEGINNER'S MIND • ZEN • NEGATIVITY NEUTRALIZER

✳ **Color** Opaque black

◎ **Born in** England, Spain, USA

☷ **Chakras** Root, 3rd Eye

◊ **Water Cleansing** ☒ Y ☐ N

MAGIC *Empty Your Mind*. Jet is a crystal to grab when you really need to clear your head. This coal-black mineral can help you connect with the magic of *shoshin*, the Zen Buddhist concept of 'Beginner's Mind,' aka dropping preconceived mindsets and assumptions so you can approach what is in front of you with fresh eyes and an open mind. Are you stuck for a solution? Or seriously lacking creative inspiration? Your mind may simply be stuffed too full; inspiration needs oxygen in order to flow, and ideas need available space in order to take root. Try giving this **Jet-Zen Meditation** a go, and see what opens up for you.

RITUAL 1) Set your timer for 10 minutes. 2) Sitting cross-legged, hold a piece of Jet in your hands, and gently focus your eyes on the floor about three feet in front of you. Focus on your breath: in and out, in and out. Whenever a thought pops into your mind, simply notice it, and let it drift on by. Keep focusing on your breath, and the spot on the floor at which you're gently staring. That's it. 3) When your timer rings, take one more deep inhale and exhale, and shake out your hands. 4) Return to what you were doing, with your newly refreshed, cleared, opened mind.

NOTES A variety of lignite coal, Jet is a lightweight organic gemstone formed from ancient driftwood that was submerged in seafloor mud. Some pieces contain metallic Pyrite inclusions. Jet jewelry was very popular during the Victorian era, particularly for mourning jewelry. **French Jet** is human-made glass.

AFFIRMATION
"My mind is open + clear"

Kunzite

DREAMS-COME-TRUE • HEART HEALING • HOPE

⊛ **Color** Translucent lilac-pink
⌖ **Born in** Afghanistan, Pakistan, Brazil
♨ **Chakras** Heart, Crown, 3rd Eye
♡ **Care** Fades in direct sunlight
◊ **Water Cleansing** ☒ Y ☐ N

MAGIC Do you remember how Glinda, the Good Witch from *The Wizard Of Oz*, instantly made everything better with her sweet presence (and that sparkly pink dress!)? Kunzite holds a similar vibration: kind, cheerful, comforting, protective, encouraging, and endlessly, unconditionally loving. *Kunzite = Your Crystal Fairy Godmother*. This very special crystal always shows up in your personal fairytale at just the right time, coming to your aid when you need protection from people or circumstances that dim your magic, and helping your tender heart heal from painful experiences that have weakened your ability to trust. Place Kunzite on your heart and let it help release the pain of the past, awaken fresh hope for the future, and empower you

to believe in yourself. Like a fairy godmother, Kunzite dissolves your fears, and helps you find the confidence to move forward towards your most magical, mystical, dreams-come-true destiny. Remember: *you are oh-so-deserving of everything good and magical!*

NOTES Kunzite is the pink variety of the mineral spodumene. The green variety (much rarer) is called **Hiddenite**. Kunzite crystallizes as long, flat crystals with vertical striations, and its color is most intense when viewed looking down its length. Larger specimens are expensive, but small raw pieces and tumbled stones are accessible and affordable. Kunzite can splinter, and fades in prolonged sunlight, so treat this crystal with care. *(koonts-ite)*

AFFIRMATION
"My dreams are coming true!"

Kyanite

CLEAR COMMUNICATION • HONESTY • ENERGY CLEARING

⊛ **Color** Pearly blue, black
◈ **Born in** Brazil, India, Nepal
⚘ **Chakras** Throat
♡ **Care** Raw pieces are brittle
◊ **Water Cleansing** ☒ Y ☐ N

MAGIC Do you often feel misunderstood or unheard? Kyanite is my go-to crystal for communication problems. With its unique crystal 'blades,' Kyanite cuts through blockages and misunderstandings, facilitating clear, direct, and compassionate communication. Sometimes hard conversations need to be had. If you know you're going into a difficult conversation or challenging meeting, bring Blue Kyanite with you; put a piece in your pocket, tuck one into your bra (polished only!), or wear it as jewelry. This communication crystal is also an excellent support stone to bring to therapy with you (and for therapists to keep in their office), as it will help you connect with your honest truth. Both blue and black Kyanite are wonderful for clearing the air after emotional conversations or arguments. Hold a crystal to your throat and take three deep belly breaths to begin to reset and rebalance. Then, wave the crystal in each corner of the room while saying *"cleanse and clear"* out loud to purify any lingering heavy vibrations. If you need extra-strength cleansing, I recommend burning your favorite ritual smoke to complete the process (palo santo is my go-to for this situation).

NOTES Kyanite is an aluminum silicate and comes in many colors, each with its own unique metaphysical qualities. Blue is the most common variety, followed by black. Fun fact for New Yorkers: the bedrock under Manhattan is full of Kyanite! Thin blades are brittle, use care; polished pieces are much more durable. Kyanite commonly forms embedded in white Quartz. *(kai-uh-nite)*

AFFIRMATION
"It is safe for me to be heard"

Labradorite

INTUITION • HONESTY • PROTECTION

✳ **Color** Gray with multicolored flash
🎯 **Born in** Madagascar, Finland, India
🪷 **Chakras** 3rd Eye, Throat
💧 **Water Cleansing** ☒ Y ☐ N

MAGIC All shades of the human eye can be seen in Labradorite's iridescent flash: blue, green, hazel, and black. I call Labradorite 'The Stone of Seeing,' as this mystical mineral helps you perceive *what is real and true in the present moment*. Intuition is a special form of seeing, and Labradorite is one of the best stones for enhancing your connection with intuition. Are you struggling with making a decision, or getting clear on a difficult situation? Hold a piece of Labradorite to your 3rd eye (*between your eyebrows*) and breathe deeply. Let your racing mind power down for a minute, and allow Labradorite to help you see below the surface of situations, relationships, and reality itself. *Be Here Now.* Labradorite also helps release your energy from things ready to evolve; everything from toxic friendships to bad habits hanging on from past lives. And its truth-revealing magic makes it a powerful stone of protection — because when you move through life as the most honest and present version of yourself, your life will feel so much more aligned, magical, and safe.

NOTES The most colorful member of the feldspar family (Moonstone is its paler cousin), Labradorite was first discovered in 1770 in Labrador, Canada, and the current largest source is the island of Madagascar. **Spectrolite** is a brand name for unusually colorful Labradorite, primarily from Finland. **Larvikite** is a dark gray variety, primarily from Norway. Labradorite mainly forms in opaque masses, and though unpolished specimens have a raw beauty, this beautiful mineral's color and iridescence is best seen once polished. *(lab-ruh-dor-ite)*

AFFIRMATION
"The truth sets me free"

Lapis Lazuli

ANCESTRAL WISDOM • GROWTH • AUTHENTICITY

✳ **Color** Blue flecked with white + gold

◎ **Born in** Afghanistan, Pakistan

🪷 **Chakras** 3rd Eye, Throat

💧 **Water Cleansing** ☐ Y ☒ N

MAGIC *Stop making excuses.* Lapis Lazuli has been treasured by royalty, priests, and holy healers for thousands of years, decorating countless precious objects with its royal-blue hue. A favorite of the ancient Egyptians, who considered it to contain immortal powers, Lapis Lazuli's magic is all about stories, histories, and authenticity. We each come from a long lineage of ancestral wisdom, and there is deep magic in the histories literally encoded into our DNA. Allow Lapis to help you access the sacred wisdom contained in your ancestral line — because by honoring the stories and lessons passed down to you, you will gain a deeper understanding of your own identity and purpose, and feel more connected with your heritage. However, it's also important to let go of old stories and attachments that may be holding you back; don't get stuck

in the past! This is where Lapis Lazuli really shines, as it helps take responsibility for your choices while still honoring the legacies that created you. Hold Lapis to your 3rd eye chakra (*between your eyebrows*) while repeating its affirmation, and it will get to work unwinding old energies that are ready to release. This is a perfect crystal to keep in areas you consider sacred (if you have an altar, this is a wonderful crystal for it), and by photos of beloved relatives. Some find it too intense to sleep near, so be thoughtful in where you keep this one. Lapis Lazuli = Helping you embrace your lineage and the wisdom it holds, so you can move forward with deeper authenticity and purpose.

NOTES Lapis Lazuli is an opaque gemstone, a combination of blue Lazurite, white Calcite, golden Pyrite, and other minerals. A rarer mineral, Sodalite and dyed Howlite and Jasper are often passed off as genuine Lapis Lazuli, but these often show more white areas, and will not have golden flecks of Pyrite. *(la-pis la-zuh-lee)*

AFFIRMATION
"I honor + integrate + transcend my past"

Larimar

FLOW · RELAXATION · TRANQUILITY

⊛ **Color** Opaque aqua + blue + white

⚑ **Born in** Dominican Republic

❀ **Chakras** Throat

♡ **Care** Fades in direct sunlight

◊ **Water Cleansing** ☒ Y ☐ N

MAGIC *Vitamin Sea.* This beautiful crystal, found only by the Caribbean Sea, swirls with cooling saltwater magic. We humans flock to water to rejuvenate, relax, and restore; there's a special level of blissed-out we reach only through spending time near water. Have you ever noticed that your problems seem much smaller and more manageable when you're looking out at the ocean horizon? *Problems shrink, possibilities expand.* Larimar helps capture that expansive feeling of tranquil possibility, and infuses you with calm vibes even when the closest shoreline is very far away. A throat-chakra crystal, Larimar will help you flow your message and magic into the world, and keeps you cool-headed when storms swirl around you. Wear this gem in jewelry to keep its soothing magic flowing throughout your day, pop a stone into your bathwater to full-body infuse yourself with its calming energy, and take a moment to simply gaze into its blue swirls whenever you need some serious chill.

NOTES A form of the mineral Pectolite, Larimar only occurs in *massive* (non-crystallized) form, and is found only in one small section of the Dominican Republic. It was named in the 1970s after the modern discoverer's daughter: Larissa (her name) + mar ('sea' in Spanish) = Larimar. Larimar is pricey, and mainly available as small slabs, tumbled stones, and polished cabochons. Also called **Atlantis Stone** and **Dolphin Stone**. *(lair-ih-mar)*

AFFIRMATION
"I flow"

Lemurian Quartz

ANCIENT WISDOM • CONSCIOUSNESS EXPANSION • ENERGY UPGRADE

✳ **Color** Crystal clear

◉ **Born in** Brazil, Colombia, Arkansas (USA)

❧ **Chakras** Crown, 3rd Eye

◇ **Water Cleansing** ☒ Y ☐ N

MAGIC Gather close, and let me tell you the unusual legend of Lemurian Quartz. Once upon a time, very long ago and very far away (*somewhere in the South Pacific?*), there was a mythical land called Lemuria. Similar to Atlantis, this ancient civilization was highly advanced both in spirit and technology, a kind of Garden of Eden. Whether through catastrophic disaster or voluntary evolution to another dimension (!), the Lemurians disappeared from the face of the earth, and their civilization sank into the murky depths of lost-continent mythology. Before they vanished, however, their wise ones 'seeded' their advanced consciousness into Quartz crystals, and these special crystals have been waiting in the earth until humanity evolved to a point where we can integrate their vibration. Now these Lemurian crystals are surfacing, infusing our reality with their consciousness-expanding wisdom and vibration. Pretty cosmic, right? Meditate with a Lemurian on your 3rd eye, or touching the top of your head, to update your personal energy system and explore consciousness expansion. Simply ask: *"What wisdom do you wish to share with me right now?"* and powerful downloads will begin. Lemurians make other crystals very happy, so definitely store these with crystalline friends to spread their energy-raising vibes.

NOTES Lemurians are Quartz crystals with horizontal, ladder-like ridges on their sides. Traditionally clear, the definition has expanded to include any Quartz crystal with horizontal ridging. Lemurians were first identified in the 1990s and originally considered to be exclusive to Brazil, but many crystal healers believe that authentic Lemurians now surface worldwide. *(leh-myur-ee-un)*

AFFIRMATION

"I channel ancient wisdom"

Lepidolite

BALANCING • COMFORTING • LIFTS DEPRESSION + ANXIETY

⊛ **Color** Silvery lilac

⚙ **Born in** Brazil

🜂 **Chakras** Heart, Crown

◊ **Water Cleansing** ☒ Y ☐ N

MAGIC *Balance*. Something we all need, so vital for functioning as a healthy human. And something we lose all too easily. Fortunately for us, silvery Lepidolite sparkles to our emotional rescue. This shimmering mica crystal is stuffed full of lithium — the same mineral used in powerful psychiatric pharmaceuticals — and is one of the best calming and stabilizing crystals for whenever life gets overwhelming. A natural antidepressant, this is a crystal to keep very close when stress, anxiety, or depression gets the upper hand. From colicky babies to overwhelmed teens, from sleep-deprived new mamas to sensitive artistic souls, absolutely everyone can benefit from Lepidolite's soothing magic. Because everyone has times when they just really, really need to hear that everything will be okay. This sweet crystal is a magic tonic for these moments. Keep one anywhere and everywhere that feels helpful. Lepidolite will help you cope with life's daily battles and challenges, so that you can shine your light into the world ever more brightly and blissfully.

NOTES Lepidolite, a lithium-rich mica mineral, forms in a variety of raw shapes, including flat slabs that peel into thin layers, and glittering scaly clusters ribboned with white Quartz. Primarily mined for industrial use, Lepidolite is one of the few minerals that contains significant amounts of lithium. *(leh-pih-doh-lite)*

AFFIRMATION
"Everything is going to be okay"

Lithium Quartz

HOLISTIC MENTAL HEALTH • ANTIDEPRESSANT • COMPASSION

✳ **Color** Dusty lilac + mauve

⊘ **Born in** Brazil

❀ **Chakras** Heart, Crown

◊ **Water Cleansing** ☒ Y ☐ N

MAGIC Lithium Quartz is a sister crystal to Lepidolite, as both contain actual lithium — the same mineral used in powerful anti-anxiety pharmaceuticals — which is what makes these crystals such magical additions to your holistic mental-health toolbox. These lilac minerals each work a bit differently. Lepidolite creates a gentle bubble of 'safe space,' very soothing for the people and energies around it. Lithium Quartz, on the other hand, helps *activate* energies to move and transform, while still maintaining a stabilizing vibration overall, which makes it wonderful at helping lift anxiety-filled or depressive vibrations from your personal aura. Lithium Quartz also helps strengthen your sense of compassion — compassion for both yourself and everyone around you — which helps you maintain grace towards

yourself and everyone you meet. As the saying goes, *"Be kind, for everyone you meet is fighting a great battle."* Lithium Quartz gently reminds you that everyone is doing their best — and that includes you, friend.

NOTES A rarer crystal, Lithium Quartz primarily comes from just one small area of Brazil. It is usually sold as small crystal points or tumbled stones. Points are usually quite imperfect, and often contain *phantoms* (transparent outlines of interior crystal points), tiny needles of the minerals Spodumene and Tourmaline, and inclusions of clay minerals such as Kaolinite. *(lih-thee-um)*

AFFIRMATION

"I give myself grace"

Lodolite

DREAMWORLD • FUTURE VISIONING • PAST LIVES

⊛ **Color** Clear with multicolored inclusions

⊘ **Born in** Brazil

⟁ **Chakras** 3rd Eye

◊ **Water Cleansing** ☒ Y ☐ N

MAGIC *Inner Worlds.* Mystical Lodolite is a crystal for vision questing, deep soul exploration, and connecting with your inner dreamworld. Swirling with multicolored magic, each Lodolite is filled with tiny details, so to truly appreciate this crystal you have to get up close and personal — a helpful reminder that up-close-and-personal is the best way to truly connect with many things. Gaze into your Lodolite crystal; let your eyes soften, your mind empty, and your breathing become deep and regular. What do you see? Images will start to dance in your inner mind, messages from your subconscious. Allow new things to come to you; what wants to rise to the surface? *What inner dreams are bubbling up from the depths of your soul?* Spend time journaling to anchor your Lodolite-inspired insights. This crystal makes a magical partner for lucid dreaming and dream journaling: keep one next to your bed (on your dream journal) to allow its insightful magic to permeate your dreamtime adventures. Lodolites that contain *phantoms* (interior shadows of a crystal point) are particularly powerful for accessing wisdom from past lives.

NOTES Lodolites are clear-to-smoky Quartz crystals with a variety of colorful mineral inclusions, including Kaolinite, Feldspar, Epidote, and Chlorite. Lodolite (also spelled Lodalite) is sold under many names, including **Dream Quartz**, **Garden Quartz**, **Inclusion Quartz**, **Landscape Quartz**, **Scenic Quartz**, and **Shaman Quartz**. **Chlorite Quartz** (green Chlorite suspended in Quartz) holds similar metaphysical gifts. *(load-oh-lite)*

AFFIRMATION
"I hear + trust the wisdom of my dreams"

Malachite

SELF-WORTH • WILLPOWER • FIDELITY

✳ **Color** Green swirls and stripes

◉ **Born in** DRC, Mexico

☙ **Chakras** Heart, Solar Plexus

◊ **Water Cleansing** Polished pieces only

MAGIC Swirling green Malachite holds powerful heart-healing energies. The active yang to Rose Quartz's gentler yin, this ancient heart crystal is an especially great gift for the special men in your life, as well as anyone who needs help with willpower, honesty, and forgiveness... and let's be honest, who couldn't use support in at least one of those areas? Holding an unusual combination of heart and solar plexus chakra energies, meditate or nap with Malachite placed on either chakra point to work through blockages related to self-worth. A powerful ally for those struggling with issues related to infidelity, honesty, and addiction, Malachite strengthens your ability to stay true to your commitments, both commitments you've made to others, and *the essential commitment of showing kindness and forgiveness to yourself*. Malachite is that no-nonsense friend everyone needs; the friend who actually calls you out on the crappy patterns you keep repeating. The friend who helps you get honest about your issues around self-worth and willpower. The friend who helps you stop holding *yourself* back from being the best, most honest, most real version of YOU possible.

NOTES Most commonly sold as polished pieces, Malachite also forms as bristly specimens sold under the names **Fibrous / Silky / Velvet Malachite**. As Malachite is a copper-based mineral it can be toxic if ingested; keep away from little mouths, and do not use in drinkable elixirs. *(mal-uh-kite)*

AFFIRMATION
"My actions are guided by the highest vibration"

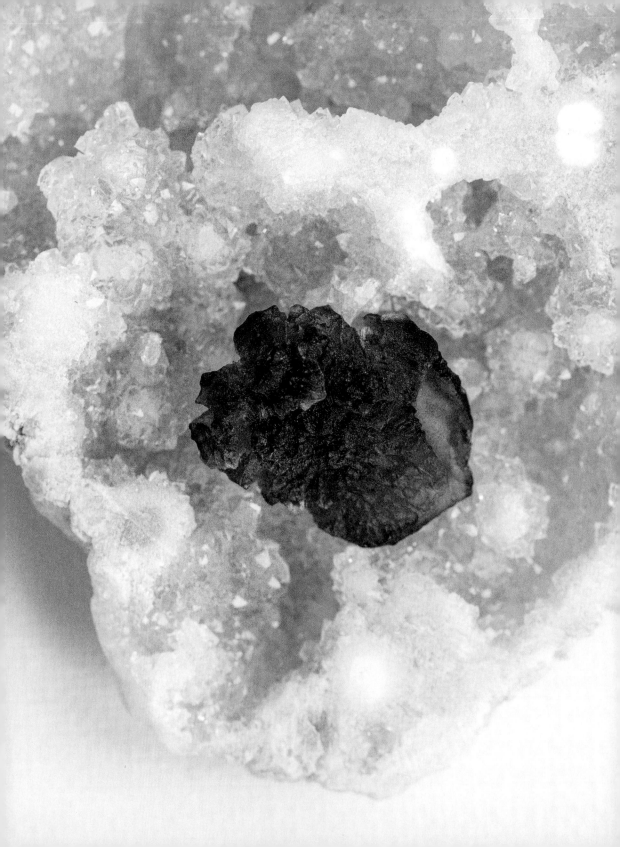

Moldavite

EXTRATERRESTRIAL • ENERGY UPGRADE • PSYCHIC JOURNEYING

✳ **Color** Glassy olive-green
🎯 **Born in** Czech Republic, Germany, Austria
☁ **Chakras** All, particularly 3rd Eye
💧 **Water Cleansing** ☒ Y ☐ N

MAGIC Of the 'modern' crystals (aka those freshly popularized by our current crystal renaissance), Moldavite hands-down has the most mystique. These small pieces of green 'space glass' formed 15 million years ago, when a huge meteorite crashed into our planet in what is now Germany. Moldavite is renowned for having extremely intense vibes, as well as an uncanny ability to mysteriously disappear and reappear at will. Many people report experiencing their first physical reaction to crystals upon touching a piece of Moldavite — heart-opening, whole-body, light-headed tingles. Because of its intense vibration, this is a crystal to work with very intentionally to avoid energetic overdosing. Begin with short sessions: hold your Moldavite in your hands, or place on your body where you feel guided (*if unsure, start with it between your eyebrows, on your 3rd eye chakra*), and simply let it work its fast-acting upgrade magic on your energy system. If you feel light-headed after spending time with Moldavite (quite common), ground yourself by standing outside on natural earth (grass, dirt, sand, etc). Moldavite can be an amazing addition to your energy toolbox, so if this crystal speaks to you, get ready to explore beyond the limits of your personal solar system!

NOTES Moldavites are tektites, a variety of mineral glass. It's thought that tektites form when rock melts due to the impact of a meteor collision, quickly cooling into small pieces of glass. Moldavite can be faceted into gemstones, however specimens are often kept in their natural form as they have such a unique look. Be aware that glass fakes are extremely common. *(mold-uh-vite)*

AFFIRMATION
"I am supernatural"

Moonstone

INTUITION • DIVINE FEMININE • MOON MAGIC

✳ **Color** White, peach, gray, black
◉ **Born in** India, Madagascar
♨ **Chakras** 3rd Eye, Sacral
◌ **Water Cleansing** ☒ Y ☐ N

MAGIC A stone of the Divine Feminine, Moonstone swirls with the intuitive magic of wise old women and magnificent mamas, ethereal goddesses and mystical mermaids. This shimmering crystal awakens radiant and empowered femininity, and will help unleash the goddess energy that flows within you (and Moonstone most certainly isn't only for women — everyone can benefit from its gifts of intuition and life-giving sensuality). Like the moon herself, glowing Moonstone is closely entwined with the ebb and flow of cycles, making this a very soothing crystal tonic for flare-ups of all types, from emotions to hormones to breakouts. Meditate with this magical gemstone placed on your 3rd eye chakra (*between your eyebrows*) or sacral chakra (*low stomach*) for cosmic intuitions, sleep with one tucked under your pillow for nighttime rebalancing, drop one into your bathwater to channel your inner mermaid, and wear Moonstone jewelry to maintain a strong connection with your intuition as you go through your day. These are also very healing crystals for fertility challenges. And don't forget to bring out your Moonstone on new and full moon nights for extra-potent, moon-magic manifesting!

NOTES A feldspar mineral, Moonstone is prized for its *adularescence*, a moonlight-like sheen. Transparent specimens with blue adularescence are the most valuable, and generally available only in antique jewelry, as the variety has essentially been mined out. The least expensive Moonstones are the opaque colored varieties. The most popular is **Rainbow Moonstone** *(pictured)*, due to its multicolored iridescence (technical fact: Rainbow Moonstone is actually a variety of Labradorite). Moonstone is a June birthstone.

AFFIRMATION
"I am guided by intuition"

Morganite

HEALTHY LOVE • RESPECT • SELF-CARE

✳ **Color** Pastel pink + peach
⊘ **Born in** Brazil, Madagascar, Afghanistan
🪷 **Chakras** Heart
💧 **Water Cleansing** ☒ Y ☐ N

MAGIC Peachy-sweet Morganite is such a lovely and nurturing heart crystal. This gentle gemstone cocoons you in the energy of a warm hug, and helps you accept only the best for yourself when it comes to matters of the heart. You deserve to be treated kindly and respectfully by everyone in your life — seriously, by 100% of the people in your life! — and Morganite lovingly reminds you of this powerful truth, empowering you to align yourself with only those who have your best intentions at heart. Boundaries are one of the biggest self-care and self-love gifts we can give ourselves. Let Morganite help you strengthen your heart's boundaries to let only truly loving vibrations in. This is a lovely crystal for friends to gift to each other, and a very healing crystal to gift to yourself when your tender heart needs nurturing

and protecting, especially after romantic breakups. Repeat Morganite's mantra as often as you need to hear it: *"I deserve to be treated with love and respect by everyone in my life."* A perfect gemstone for honoring a commitment to loving with kindness and mutual respect, Morganite has recently become one of the most popular options for engagement rings.

NOTES The pink variety of beryl, Morganite is a sister crystal to Emerald and Aquamarine. It is sometimes sold under the names **Pink Emerald** / **Pink Beryl** / **Rose Beryl**. Morganite was first identified in 1910 in Madagascar, and was named by Tiffany & Co. after the wealthy industrialist (and passionate gem collector) J.P. Morgan. *(mor-guh-nite)*

AFFIRMATION
"I deserve to be treated with love + respect by everyone in my life"

Obsidian

ENERGY SHIELDING • PROTECTION • GRIEVING

Color Varies according to variety
Born in USA, Mexico
Chakras Root
Water Cleansing ☒ Y ☐ N

MAGIC Formed by powerful volcanic eruptions, Obsidian is a stone of protection and divination. A natural glass whose edges can be sharper than a steel knife, Obsidian's #1 gift is energy deflection. It wraps an impenetrable energetic shield around you, making this a valuable protection talisman for sensitive souls and emotional empaths. Holding a piece in your hand, imagine a jet-black shield rising up between you and the source of your worry or fear. Use this magic wisely, however; an Obsidian shield is very useful in circumstances that can overwhelm your nervous system, such as large crowds. But this probably isn't the crystal to take with you to social gatherings, as it will shield your energy from connecting with others, very likely making you feel invisible. **Apache Tears**, a rounded variety found in the American Southwest, is one of the best crystals for processing grief and loss. Obsidian is also a crystal of *divination* (the mystical art of seeing the future) and is very useful when you need help making difficult decisions. Hold a crystal in your hand, quiet your mind, and observe what materializes in your inner mind. You'll know what to do.

NOTES Obsidian forms in several varieties, black being the most common and affordable. **Snowflake Obsidian** has inclusions of white Cristobalite; **Mahogany Obsidian** has inclusions of red Hematite; **Sheen Obsidian** has tiny water vapor bubble inclusions, creating a sparkling shimmer; **Rainbow Obsidian** includes nanoparticles of the mineral Hedenbergite, creating a stunning rainbow shimmer. Note that several colors of human-made transparent glass are commonly sold as 'Obsidian' varieties (**Aqua Obsidian** is a popular one). *(uhb-sid-ee-yin)*

AFFIRMATION
"I am shielded"

Onyx / Sardonyx

STRENGTH • PROTECTION • ANXIETY SOOTHING

✳ **Color** Black, brown, white, red

⚬ **Born in** India, Brazil, Uruguay

♡ **Chakras** Root, Sacral

💧 **Water Cleansing** ☒ Y ☐ N

MAGIC Onyx and Sardonyx are ancient healing crystals for strengthening your inner soul-core. Worn by Roman warriors for strength in battle, add one to your crystal toolkit for assistance with grounding and stabilizing when life's seas get choppy. These gemstones can help quiet overactive mind-chatter, worry, anxiety, and fear. Place one under your pillow to keep anxiety-fueled nightmares away, and wear Onyx jewelry to keep yourself grounded throughout your day. This is a great stone for kids to help calm hyperactivity and anxiety. Onyx's name comes from the Greek word for fingernail, *onux*, and originates in an odd ancient myth. Eros, god of love and sex, mischievously cut the fingernails of his goddess mother, Aphrodite, with an arrowhead while she slept. Her fingernail clippings sank to the bottom of a nearby river, and since no part of a deity can decay, they transformed into beautiful, white-banded stones: Onyx. Onyx has black and white bands, while Sardonyx has red, brown, and white bands. Both varieties have been carved into intricate cameos and intaglios since antiquity.

NOTES Onyx and Sardonyx are varieties of Chalcedony. Mineralogically identical to Agate, the difference lies in the shape of their bands: traditional Agate has curved bands, while Onyx and Sardonyx have straighter bands (Onyx can also be solid black). The majority of 'Onyx' sold today is actually banded Calcite or Alabaster (such as **Cave Onyx**, **Mexican Onyx**, **Onyx Marble**). Pure-black Onyx is often artificially dyed, so if you don't resonate with dyed stones be sure to buy from a trusted source. *(aw-nicks)*

AFFIRMATION
"I am strong + protected"

Common Opal

HEART BOOST • FRESH ENERGY • UPLIFTING

✳ **Color** A variety of bright shades

◎ **Born in** Peru, Madagascar

🪷 **Chakras** Heart

💧 **Water Cleansing** ☒ Y ☐ N

MAGIC Although these Opals don't swirl with stunning rainbows like their better-known siblings (the 'Precious' Opals), they are very sweet crystals to add to your collection, and much more affordable. You know how sometimes just a little taste of something sweet provides the perfect pick-me-up to continue on with fresh energy? I find these bright Opals have a similar uplifting effect, especially on matters of the heart; they're like little candies for your heart chakra! A lovely way to work with them is to place one on your chest (*heart chakra*) for five minutes, while you breathe calmly and allow yourself to gently recharge. You don't have to 'do' anything — just let these sweet crystals work their happy, pastel magic. We process so, so much through our heart, so giving it a boost of crystalline support is always a great idea. **Dendritic Opal**, a variety with delicate, moss-like inclusions, helps you remember that everything is interconnected, and trust that you will always be supported and nurtured — you are held in the web of life.

NOTES These brightly colored crystals are varieties of 'common' Opal, as they do not show rainbow flash. They form worldwide in a range of colors, and are often sold as tumbled stones. Some green varieties are called **Prase Opal** or **Chrysopal**, as they can look similar to Chrysoprase. Bright Opals from Peru are sold under the names **Andean Opal** and **Peruvian Opal**. Opals are an October birthstone. *(oh-pull)*

AFFIRMATION
"My heart is recharged"

Precious Opal

MYSTICISM • MAGIC • EMBRACE THE PROCESS

✳ **Color** Varies according to variety

◈ **Born in** Australia, Ethiopia, Mexico

❀ **Chakras** 3rd Eye

♡ **Care** Can crack in prolonged sun

◊ **Water Cleansing** ☐ Y ☒ N

MAGIC These mystical gemstones hide endless rainbows within their depths. To see them, all you have to do is shift slightly, and shimmering colors suddenly dance to life. *Looking + Shifting + Believing = MAGIC*. Precious Opal is a reminder to look beyond the surface. Look deeper, look closer: at people, places, ideas, and (most importantly) within yourself. Historically treasured as a talisman of loyalty and faithfulness, this gemstone also reminds us to trust the process. Opals take thousands of years to form, so they know a thing or two about perseverance, patience, and not getting bogged down in the small stuff — because when you're thousands of years old, it's all small stuff. Let Opal help you trust that everything happens in the right time, you're exactly where you're meant to be, and you're surrounded by magic at all times. This is a power stone for all you magic-makers and magic-believers — anyone who trusts that mystery dances around every corner, 'reality' isn't only what can be seen at first glance, and magic is very, very real.

NOTES Opals form very slowly, over thousands of years, from evaporated silica water. Occurring worldwide in many colors, only the 'precious' varieties show the rainbow flash called play-of-color. **White Opal**, **Black Opal**, **Boulder Opal**, and **Fire Opal** are the best-known precious varieties, and the vast majority comes from the wild Australian outback. A fragile mineral, gemstones are often stabilized, and synthetics are commonly used for inexpensive jewelry. **Opalite** is human-made glass. Opals are an October birthstone. (<u>oh</u>-pull)

AFFIRMATION
"Magic flows to me + through me"

Peacock Ore

PLAY • INNER CHILD • CREATIVITY

⊛ **Color** Metallic rainbow

◎ **Born in** Mexico, USA

❀ **Chakras** All

◊ **Water Cleansing** ☐ Y ☒ N

MAGIC Named for its resemblance to jewel-toned peacock feathers, this is often the first crystal that mini rock collectors (aka the kids!) reach for. Peacock Ore's appeal to little ones goes beyond its cool surface shimmer, however, as this rainbow crystal holds energies of light-hearted fun, playfulness, and exploration — exactly what kids are so naturally magnificent at embodying, and something most of us adults could benefit from prioritizing more. Remember how good it felt to stomp in the mud, cover yourself with paint, play dress-up for hours, and generally run around living life with absolutely zero worries given for what was 'normal' or 'cool?' You don't have to go to Burning Man to experience this childlike freedom again — Peacock Ore can help you reconnect with your fun-loving inner child, and infuse a sense of creative play into your everyday. Whenever you see your Peacock Ore, remember its permission-granting mantra: *"I allow myself to play and explore; that's where the rainbow-colored magic lives!"*

NOTES Peacock Ore is a popular name for oxidized **Chalcopyrite** and / or **Bornite**, both of which are copper ore minerals. When they undergo a natural oxidation process, they develop a colorful, iridescent surface. Inexpensive Peacock Ore has most likely been treated with acid to magnify its colors. Untreated Chalcopyrite is commonly confused with Pyrite, as they are both metallic-yellow minerals.

AFFIRMATION
"I allow myself to play + explore"

Pearl

TRANSFORMATION • PROTECTION • FERTILITY

⊛ **Color** Iridescent pastels
⌖ **Born in** Worldwide
♋ **Chakras** Heart
◊ **Water Cleansing** ☒ Y ☐ N

MAGIC Luminous Pearls are the only gemstones formed by a living creature. First, an 'invader' (usually a grain of sand or tiny parasite) enters the shell of a bivalve mollusk, a soft-bodied invertebrate who lives inside shells. The mollusk then protects itself by coating the foreign object over and over with a silky substance, which over time hardens into an iridescent pearl. *Transformation.* Pearls are very special reminders that our most difficult experiences often become our most luminous, precious parts; it just takes time — and dedicated soulwork — to transform a challenge into glowing radiance. Wear Pearl jewelry to remind yourself that you are strong enough to transcend any challenge that comes your way. A protective gemstone, Pearl can encase you in a bubble of protection, another reason to wear this gemstone in jewelry. Pearls can also harness extra-potent moon magic: place one overnight in the light of a new or full moon, with a prayer that your troubles be luminously transformed. *Expect transformation.* These are time-honored talismans for fertility, so I recommend keeping one close if you are calling in a spirit baby.

NOTES Pearls are primarily composed of the mineral Aragonite. As 'natural' Pearls (formed without human help) are extremely rare, most pearls are 'cultured,' grown in human-tended mollusks. Pearls form in both freshwater and seawater, and in a wide variety of colors. **Mother of Pearl** and **Abalone** are the pearlized lining of shells. Imitation Pearls are extremely common; to check if your Pearl is organic or imitation, rub it lightly against the front of your tooth. Gritty = natural or cultured, smooth = imitation. Pearl is a June birthstone.

AFFIRMATION
"I trust + transcend"

Peridot

SELF-ESTEEM • INDIVIDUALISM • ABUNDANCE

⊛ **Color** Lime green

⚲ **Born in** USA, Pakistan, Myanmar

❀ **Chakras** Solar Plexus, Heart, 3rd Eye

◊ **Water Cleansing** ☒ Y ☐ N

MAGIC Bright Peridot is a gemstone of individualism, strong boundaries, and healthy self-esteem. This crystal often appeals to people who like to 'go their own way': the non-conformists, rebels, and boundary-pushers. Peridot encourages you to develop strong boundaries and the ability to stand confidently in your choices, even when they go against the norm. *You do you.* Often found in areas of volcanic activity, Peridot is associated with Pele, fierce Hawaiian goddess of fire and volcanoes. Just as a volcano or fire burns everything in its path, Peridot can help clear away energies that are holding you back, such as jealousy, insecurity, and indecision. Place this crystal on your body in spots where you feel you need some clarity and fresh energy. Just be aware that this crystal can increase stubbornness, so if you know that's a pattern for you, pay attention and make sure you're keeping an open mind (especially while wearing Peridot jewelry). A beloved ancient gemstone for luck, Peridot can also help you tap into a flow of abundance due to its cleansing powers — because you've first gotta get rid of the old to make room for the new!

NOTES Peridot is the gem-quality form of the mineral **Olivine,** and is most commonly available as small tumbled chips, and faceted or cabochon gemstones. Peridot is an August birthstone. *(pear-uh-doh or pear-uh-dot)*

AFFIRMATION
"I dance to my beat!"

Petrified Wood

TRUST • PATIENCE • GROWTH

✳ **Color** Opaque brown, gray, red, yellow

⌖ **Born in** Worldwide

⚘ **Chakras** Root

◇ **Water Cleansing** ☒ Y ☐ N

MAGIC There is a profound wisdom we can access when we allow ourselves to *simply be present*, no matter how challenging the moment, and Petrified Wood is a special talisman of this wisdom. This fossilized wood has been transformed by time and pressure into something even more durable and beautiful than its original form, and is a reminder that even in the face of adversity, we too can remain strong and resilient — transforming into something even stronger than what we were before. As the wise Serenity Prayer reminds us, although we cannot always change the circumstance of our lives, we can always change how we respond. Petrified Wood will help you grow deeper roots, so that you can tap into your own inner strength for stability in times of change. So embrace your inner treehugger,

and allow Petrified Wood to support you on your journey towards greater serenity and courage. Let it be a reminder that even in the midst of change, there is great beauty, growth, and wisdom to be found.

NOTES A fossilized form of wood where all organic materials have been replaced with minerals over millions of years, Petrified Wood is primarily composed of silica-based minerals such as Chalcedony and Opal. Formed from wood buried in water or volcanic ash, it is found worldwide in a variety of colors and patterns.

AFFIRMATION
*"Grant me serenity to accept the things I cannot change,
courage to change the things I can, and wisdom to know the difference"*

Prehnite

EXTRATERRESTRIAL • PROBLEM SOLVING • ALKALINIZING

✳ **Color** Translucent green

☉ **Born in** Australia, China, South Africa

⚭ **Chakras** Solar Plexus, 3rd Eye

♡ **Care** Fades in direct sunlight

◊ **Water Cleansing** ☒ Y ☐ N

MAGIC Prehnite has a kind of otherworldly vibration, so if you're one of those people drawn to all things extraterrestrial — aliens, UFOs, perhaps those fascinating Pleiadians? — Prehnite should be a very interesting crystal for you to add to your collection. Meditate with a piece on your 3rd eye *(between your eyebrows)* to tap into otherworldly transmissions and communications, and to change your vibration to a range where contact is more plausible. Also holding a left-brain, problem-solving energy, this is a great crystal ally for when you need to double down on analytical activities, from science homework to income taxes. On the health front, this lime-green crystal is helpful for the digestive system, as it carries a cleansing form of solar plexus energy; I like to think of it as an alkalinizing glass of lime water in crystal form. Place a Prehnite on your solar plexus chakra *(above your belly button)*, or wear Prehnite jewelry when you feel the need for a boost of freshness, both in health and spirit. Whether you're seeking to connect with otherworldly beings or simply looking for a natural way to enhance your health and wellbeing, Prehnite is a crystal worth exploring!

NOTES Often crystallizing in globular clusters, Prehnite is most commonly sold as tumbled stones, cabochons, and faceted beads. Until quite recently Prehnite was a rare collector's mineral, but the discovery of new sources have made it affordable. Prehnite forms in shades of tan and yellow, as well as green. Many specimens show embedded dark mineral 'threads,' usually Epidote. *(pray-nite or preh-nite)*

AFFIRMATION
"I am clear + refreshed"

Pyrite

ABUNDANCE • CONFIDENCE • MANIFESTATION

✷ **Color** Metallic gold

⬦ **Born in** Peru, Spain

☸ **Chakras** Solar plexus

💧 **Water Cleansing** ☐ Y ☒ N

MAGIC *Go for gold.* A crystal of supercharged abundance and get-it-done productivity, golden Pyrite is a powerhouse of confidence, action, and luck. Given its name by the ancient Greeks upon discovering that striking Pyrite on steel sparks literal fire, this metallic mineral continues to ignite major magic for us modern crystal lovers. One of the best crystals to increase self-confidence, this solar plexus crystal will help burn through procrastination and self-doubt, giving you fresh courage to take action on sharing your unique gifts with the world. To give a megaboost to your confidence and abundance vibration, hold Pyrite to your belly and spend a few minutes in your favorite good-vibes activity — listening to positive affirmations, dancing to good music,

writing a gratitude list, whatever's your go-to for raising your energy. *This is core power for your soul*. One of my personal favorites, don't say I didn't warn you when creative inspirations, dream collaborations, and lucky breaks start manifesting with miraculous abundance after you bring this powerhouse crystal into your life!

NOTES An iron-based mineral, Pyrite crystallizes in a variety of glittering forms. Widespread worldwide, most specimens come from Peru, and Spanish Pyrite is prized for its perfect cubes. Pyrite has earned the nickname **Fool's Gold** by misleading countless gold hunters, as it is often found side-by-side with the real thing. Pyrite dulls when exposed to moisture, so don't leave outside overnight. Small Pyrite crystals can form on many other minerals, adding a dose of abundance magic to the host crystal's overall vibration. *(pie-right)*

AFFIRMATION
"Unlimited abundance flows to me + through me"

Rhodochrosite

DIVINE FEMININE • MOTHERING LOVE • HEART HEALING

✳ **Color** Swirls of rose + white

♂ **Born in** Argentina, Peru, USA

🫀 **Chakras** Heart

💧 **Water Cleansing** ☒ Y ☐ N

MAGIC *You are Unconditionally Loved.* Swirling with elegant bands of pink and white, Rhodochrosite is an unfurling rose in crystal form. Named after the ancient Greek word for rose, this pink crystal holds a powerful energy of Unconditional Love, similar to the energy represented by many holy figures — including the Virgin Mary, who is often symbolized by a rose. This rosy gemstone is the perfect support crystal for times when you deeply need 'mothering,' a non-judgmental, unconditional variety of mothering. Hold Rhodochrosite to your heart, and let yourself feel completely held in the most gentle, safe embrace imaginable. Feel the essence of the Divine Mother (whatever that term personally means to you) holding you, loving you, saying softly: *"My sweet one, let the walls around your heart soften. I am always right here with you. You are so safe. You are so loved. You are Divinely, Unconditionally Loved."* Allow yourself to feel held. Allow yourself to feel mothered. Allow yourself to feel so, so loved. (And PS: don't be surprised if you suddenly sense the distinct fragrance of roses when healing with Rhodochrosite!)

NOTES Rhodochrosite is often confused with its crystal sister, Rhodonite, due to their similar names and pink swirls. To easily tell the difference, remember that Rhodochrosite rarely has black inclusions, while Rhodonite almost always does. Rhodochrosite is most commonly available as polished pieces and tumbled stones; crystallized specimens are quite rare and pricey. *(ro-do-croh-site)*

AFFIRMATION
"I am unconditionally loved"

Rhodonite

LETTING GO • HEARTBREAK TONIC • BOUNDARIES

✳ **Color** Swirls of rose + black + white
⊘ **Born in** Peru, Madagascar, Canada
⚘ **Chakras** Heart, Root
◌ **Water Cleansing** ☒ Y ☐ N

MAGIC First discovered in the late 1700s in the Urals, a mystical mountain range in Russia, Rhodonite was given the name 'Eagle Stone' by locals, upon witnessing the phenomenon of eagles carrying small pieces of this pink crystal back to their nests. Eagles are animal totems of courage, wisdom, and strength, and Rhodonite holds a similarly protective, boundary-strengthening vibration. This pink-swirled stone is a balm for deep heart healing and grief releasing. A stabilizing tonic for heartbreak, Rhodonite is a valuable crystal ally for difficult transitions of all kinds, from relationship and career changes, to illness and death. When you need support processing something challenging, place Rhodonite on your heart, breathe deeply, and allow the cracks in your heart to be filled with healing and light. Rhodonite helps release stuck, fearful energies related to self-worth and self-love, and will help you establish much healthier boundaries around your heart.

NOTES Rhodonite is most commonly found in *massive* (non-crystallized) form, and sold in a variety of polished pieces. Crystallized clusters are rare and pricey. Rhodonite is often confused with Rhodochrosite due to their similar rose-white swirls; Rhodonite can be identified by its black inclusions of manganese dioxide. *(roh-doh-nite)*

AFFIRMATION
"My heart is strong + protected"

Rose Quartz

LOVE • KINDNESS • COMPASSION

✳ **Color** Translucent rosy pink

◎ **Born in** Madagascar, Brazil

❀ **Chakras** Heart

♡ **Care** Fades in direct sunlight

◊ **Water Cleansing** ☒ Y ☐ N

MAGIC *All you need is love.* With its soft cotton-candy hue, Rose Quartz may seem delicate at first glance, but don't be fooled; this is one of the most empowering and nurturing crystals of the entire crystal realm! The ultimate love crystal, Rose Quartz is legendary for its ability to heal heartbreak, attract new romance, and open hearts to new levels of compassion, forgiveness, and *love, love, love*. All of life's many forms of love — romantic, family, self-love, Universal — are strengthened by this absolutely magical crystal. Rose Quartz is the crystal I personally turn to more than any other, and I keep pieces stashed just about everywhere for easy access to 'love booster shots.' To gift yourself a dose, simply hold a Rose Quartz to your heart and visualize a soft pink light filling your heart space, melting all heaviness and heartache away. *Heart-healing magic.* Everyone can benefit from Rose Quartz's beautiful vibration, so keep these rosy crystals anywhere and everywhere — the more Rose Quartz in your life, the Lovelier!

NOTES Rose Quartz is a pink variety of Quartz. It is almost always found in 'massive' form without crystal terminations, which is broken down and sold in a huge variety of raw and polished shapes. The majority of Rose Quartz comes from the African island of Madagascar. Crystallized Rose Quartz clusters are rare and expensive, so if you see one sold relatively cheaply it's most likely artificially dyed.

AFFIRMATION
"I am Love"

Ruby

POWER • PASSION • PROTECTION

✳ **Color** Shades of red
◎ **Born in** Myanmar, Sri Lanka, East Africa
🪷 **Chakras** Root, Sacral, Heart
💧 **Water Cleansing** ☒ Y ☐ N

MAGIC Treasured by ancient emperors, Renaissance alchemists, and Hollywood stars alike, Rubies are one of humanity's favorite gemstones, prized throughout history for their combination of physical beauty and intense metaphysical magic. Supremely protective and grounding, Ruby resonates with our two lower chakras, helping clear deeply rooted issues related to self-worth, scarcity, and survival — and we've all got *plenty* of those to work through during this lifetime. So spend time with a Ruby placed right below your tailbone (between your thighs) for help working through old patterns and stagnant energies — meditating and / or sleeping with Ruby is a great way to integrate its magic. Ruby jewelry is powerfully talismanic; wear it to remind you of your innate power, life-force, and strength.

This gemstone is also great for spicing up all facets of your love life — keep one close to your heart for romantic love (wear a Ruby necklace, or slip a small crystal into your bra), and tuck one under your mattress for passionate bedroom fire. And last — but definitely not least — keep this beloved abundance crystal in spots you associate with money. There's nothing like opening your wallet and seeing a little Ruby rattling around to make you feel like a high-roller!

NOTES The red form of the mineral corundum (Sapphire is its blue-hued sister), quality Rubies are one of the most expensive gemstones, but opaque raw crystals and tumbled stones are affordable. Often crystallizing as flat hexagonal crystals, **Record-Keeper Ruby** is a variety that shows triangular markings, said to contain ancient metaphysical knowledge *(pictured)*. Ruby can form blended with several green-blue minerals; turn the page to learn more. Ruby is a July birthstone.

AFFIRMATION
"I am powerful"

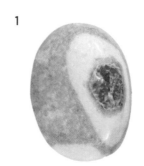

RUBY BLENDS:

1) RUBY FUCHSITE *(Rubies enclosed in a blue band of Kyanite, blended with green Fuchsite)* A gentle crystal connected to holistic healing, nature, and the elemental world, Ruby Fuchsite helps open you to the deep wisdom contained within plants and nature, while still keeping you rooted so you don't float off into fairyland (aka lose your sense of grounding). *Chakras: Root, Heart*

2) RUBY ZOISITE *(Ruby blended with emerald-green Zoisite, usually speckled with black Amphibole)* Ruby Zoisite helps ground your emotions in the present moment, aka it helps you get honest, realistic, and truthful about what is *actually* going on, so you don't get stuck in mind games, especially related to relationships and sex. Also called **Anyolite**. *Chakras: Root, Heart*

3) RUBY KYANITE *(Ruby blended with blue Kyanite)* Kyanite is a stone of truth-telling and healthy communication. This crystal helps you stay grounded while communicating your truth with clarity, bravery, and power. The rarest of these combo crystals. *Chakras: Root, Throat*

Rutilated Quartz

HOPE • ANGELIC ASSISTANCE • ENERGY ZAPS

✳ **Color** Clear with golden / copper fibers

◎ **Born in** Brazil

✿ **Chakras** Solar Plexus, Crown

◊ **Water Cleansing** ☒ Y ☐ N

MAGIC Filled with shimmering strands of titanium, Rutilated Quartz holds a vibration of hope-filled optimism and positivity. Just like the fairytale moral of Rapunzel, that golden-haired damsel in distress, this happy mineral helps remind us to *never give up hope*, no matter how dark or difficult our current circumstances. If you're struggling with depression or a general lack of energy, Rutilated Quartz is a great crystal for giving yourself uplifting energy 'zaps': place one above your belly button *(solar plexus chakra)* and let it work its anti-depressive, energizing magic. It's also great for making energizing water elixirs *(see page 47).* And keep Rutilated Quartz close when you feel completely overwhelmed, as this crystal connects you with angelic assistance. For a supercharged infusion of celestial support, place eight crystals in a circle around your body and lie quietly, breathing deeply, for at least 10 minutes. I guarantee that you'll be flying much higher by the time you finish.

NOTES Rutilated Quartz forms when Quartz encases hairlike strands of Rutile, a form of titanium oxide. Inclusions range from golden to coppery-brown, with bright gold the most common and popular color. Natural underground radiation can darken specimens to create **Rutilated Smoky Quartz**, a less common variety. Historic names include **Venus Hairstone** and **Cupid's Darts**. Also called **Rutile Quartz**. *(roo-tuh-lay-ted)*

AFFIRMATION
"I am uplifted"

Sapphire

BIG-PICTURE VISION • COMPASSION • LOYALTY

⊛ **Color** Blue, yellow, clear, pink +

⌀ **Born in** Sri Lanka, Madagascar, Myanmar +

♋ **Chakras** Throat, 3rd Eye

◌ **Water Cleansing** ☒ Y ☐ N

MAGIC *Do The Right Thing.* Revered as 'The Wisdom Stone' since ancient times, Sapphire helps you connect with your Higher Self: your inner empath who sees the bigger picture, acts from a global perspective, and can imagine walking in someone else's shoes (in other words, the part of you which makes choices for the best of *everyone* involved). In our modern age, Sapphire is most associated with Princess Diana, who had a special love for this crystal, choosing a deep blue gemstone for her iconic engagement ring. It makes perfect sense that she was drawn to Sapphire, as this is a powerful crystal ally for humanitarians, altruists, philanthropists, and do-gooders of all levels, from local heroes to global humanitarian icons like Diana. Keep Sapphire close to help you stretch your compassion muscles, empower your better

self, and keep small-minded, fear-based thinking at bay. *Be the change you wish to see in the world.*

NOTES Sapphires are the mineral corundum. The hardest mineral on earth after Diamonds, corundum forms in a multitude of colors, all of which are known as varieties of Sapphire except one color: red Rubies. Blue is by far the best-known variety of Sapphire, and ranges from inexpensive tumbled stones to priceless gemstones. Sapphire is a September birthstone.

AFFIRMATION
"I am the change I wish to see in the world"

Scolecite

EMPATH PROTECTION • INNER PEACE • ACCEPTANCE

✳ **Color** Clear, white, pink
◎ **Born in** India, Iceland, Brazil
❧ **Chakras** Crown, 3rd Eye
💧 **Water Cleansing** ☒ Y ☐ N

MAGIC Scolecite is a space-holding crystal. Tumbled stones look like pillowy marshmallows, and just like little pillows, these white crystals act as crystalline buffers to help pad you from energetic overwhelm. You're going to love Scolecite if you feel a lot of empathy, aka if you're deeply sensitive to the energies and emotions of other people. It's very important to protect your *own* energy and boundaries, so I highly recommend adding this crystal to your toolkit to gift yourself its ability to create a gentle buffer of crystalline protection around you. Scolecite holds space for you to simply BE. It helps you release attachment to outcomes, and helps you relax into a state of calm acceptance, opening the energetic space for what is truly best to magically manifest. Wonderful for soothing anxiety and overactive minds. Scolecite is a great crystal to keep near your bed (on your nightstand / under your pillow / tucked under your mattress) to help you fall into deep, calm sleep.

NOTES Scolecite is in the zeolite family, a group of more than 40 water-containing silicate minerals (Stilbite and Tanzanite are the other zeolites featured in this book). Scolecite is usually clear or white, and more uncommonly pink, red, or green. (*sko*-leh-site or *skah*-leh-site)

AFFIRMATION
"My energy + boundaries are protected"

Selenite

CLEANSING • CLEARING • MOON MAGIC

✳ **Color** Translucent white

◎ **Born in** Morocco, Mexico, USA

♨ **Chakras** Crown, 3rd Eye

◊ **Water Cleansing** ☐ Y ☒ N

MAGIC Named after Selene, Greek goddess of the moon, Selenite is a must-have crystal for keeping your aura fresh and sparkling *(aura = your personal energy sphere)*. These moonbeam crystals are the ultimate crystal tool for cleansing and clearing the energy of auras, physical spaces, and even other crystals. I highly recommend keeping a Selenite near your front door so you can give yourself a quick energy rinse when you return home at the end of a long day. Simply wave the Selenite around the edges of your body (don't forget your back!), and it will wipe you clear from any sticky vibes that may have latched on while you were out and about. *Be clear, be bright, be radiant.* There are a myriad of other ways to add Selenite's purifying magic to your daily life. Some ideas: store a piece in your refrigerator and cupboards to keep food high-vibe and fresh; Selenite in bedrooms helps calm restless sleepers and keeps nightmares away; keeping a larger piece near computers, televisions, and routers helps balance disruptive electrical discharge. When your other crystals feel like they need an energy refresh, you can place them on a piece of Selenite for a few hours to recharge (this is my go-to technique for refreshing jewelry). And be sure to add a Selenite crystal to your new and full moon rituals for potent moon-magic manifesting!

NOTES Selenite is a form of the mineral gypsum. A soft mineral, it scratches easily, and should not be exposed to water. It's available in a wide variety of shapes and sizes; flat pieces ideal for cleansing other crystals and jewelry are often sold as Selenite plates or wands. Orange-colored specimens, a rarer variety, are sold as **Peach / Orange / Red Selenite**. *(sell-uh-nite)*

AFFIRMATION
"I am cleansed + cleared"

Serpentine

RELEASE OLD PATTERNS • EMBRACE CHANGE • PROTECTION

✳ **Color** Opaque shades of green

◎ **Born in** Worldwide

☯ **Chakras** Solar Plexus, Heart

◊ **Water Cleansing** ☒ Y ☐ N

MAGIC *The only constant is change*. Named for their visual and tactile resemblance to waxy-cool snakeskin, Serpentine minerals have been prized worldwide since ancient times. Serpents are one of our most potent animal totems, symbolizing rebirth and the shedding of old to make way for new. These crystals can help you release fears and resistance when you are in intense periods of transition — *when you are shedding your outdated skin*. Releasing old patterns and being rebirthed in a new, upgraded version can be intensely vulnerable, so lean on Serpentine when you need deep support. To easily infuse yourself with its energy, place a stone in your bathwater while you soak. Serpentine is an ancient protection talisman — put it in the four corners of your home to connect with the protective nature spirits of the land on which your home is built, and bring a stone with you when you travel to help you ground into the energy of new locations. Serpentine will help you feel more at home wherever you are.

NOTES The name 'Serpentine' technically refers both to a family of minerals and the specific variety featured here. There are many names used for Serpentine varieties in the crystal healing world, with a lot of confusing overlap. Some guidance: **Lizardite** is an alternate name for the most abundant variety of Serpentine; **Precious / Noble Serpentine** is used for specimens that have a higher quality of color and durability; **Bowenite** is a variety that is extra hard; **Healerite** is an alternate name for Serpentine from the Northwestern US; **Infinite** is gray-green Serpentine; **Atlantisite** is Serpentine + purple stichtite. Serpentine is also sold as 'Jade' under many names, including **New / Korean / Lemon Jade** *(psst: your 'jade' face roller is almost definitely Serpentine!)*. (*ser*-pen-teen)

AFFIRMATION

"It is safe for me to transform"

Shungite

DETOX • PURIFY • PROTECTION

✳ **Color** Metallic black

⚲ **Born in** Russia

♋ **Chakras** Root

💧 **Water Cleansing** ☒ Y ☐ N

MAGIC *Primordial magic*. A carbon rock formed billions of years ago from ancient algae (!), Shungite has quite the reputation as a health cure-all, especially when used in water elixirs. However, it is very important to be aware that Shungite is available in two distinct varieties that should be used differently, and it's also vital that you get your Shungite from a source you trust, as imitation Shungite can contain lead and other substances you definitely don't want to ingest. **Black Shungite** (also called **Classic Shungite**) has a dull black sheen, and is the more common and affordable variety. Often ground up and reformed into polished shapes such as tumbled stones, pyramids, and beads, this form of Shungite usually contains a low level of carbon (35% or less), and should *not* be used in water elixirs. Instead, you can place it around your home and electronics for energy neutralization and protection, meditate with it on your body for detoxification, and it's a wonderful crystal to use in protection grids. Rarer, more expensive **Silver Shungite** (also called **Noble / Elite Shungite**) has a metallic sheen, and is only available in raw pieces as it isn't durable enough to be polished *(pictured)*. Composed primarily of pure carbon, this form of Shungite is the one to use in water elixirs, and is scientifically proven to have antibacterial and antioxidant properties. Place one piece (or more) in a jug of water, steep for at least a few hours, and drink to your health!

NOTES Shungite is found almost exclusively in the Karelia region of western Russia, bordering Finland. Shungite is an electricity conductor, and it is possible to check the authenticity and carbon content of Shungite yourself with a multimeter. Fun fact: in the early 1700s, czar Peter the Great established the first Russian spa in Karelia, due to the water-purifying properties of Shungite. *(shun-gite)*

AFFIRMATION

"I detox from everything ready to release"

Silver

PROTECTION • MOON MAGIC • FERTILITY

⊛ **Color** Metallic silver

🜨 **Born in** Worldwide

☙ **Chakras** Crown, 3rd Eye

◇ **Water Cleansing** ☐ Y ☒ N

MAGIC In astrology, your Moon Sign represents your inner world: your emotions, your moods, your deepest feelings. Silver, the 'moon metal,' holds a similar vibration to that represented by moon signs, as this silvery mineral is also deeply connected to emotions, intuition, and inner knowledge. Associated since ancient times with feminine energy and a multitude of goddesses, jewelry made with Silver often appeals to introverts and sensitive souls, as it creates a gentle energy 'cocoon' around you while you go through your daily life — a personal safe space. When you put on your Silver jewelry in the morning, say its affirmation to connect yourself with its protective magic — *"I am safe and protected"* — and as you go through your day, imagine yourself surrounded by a silvery, moonlike bubble

whenever you feel the need to reconnect with its protective vibration. Leave your Silver jewelry overnight in a moonlit spot once a month to cleanse and recharge its energy. Silver is also a deeply respected ancient talisman of fertility and motherhood; I recommend wearing Silver jewelry when you are hoping to conceive.

NOTES One of the precious metals, pure Silver is an element (*Ag*). It is a soft mineral, so it is combined with other minerals to increase its durability for jewelry and other objects. The standard mix is 'sterling', or '925' = 92.5% pure Silver + 7.5% other minerals, usually Copper. It is the Copper content that causes sterling silver to tarnish, as Copper oxidizes when exposed to water.

AFFIRMATION
"I am safe + protected"

Smoky Quartz

ENERGY CLEANSING · STRESS RELIEF · GROUNDING

⊛ **Color** Translucent brown + gray

♂ **Born in** Worldwide

🪷 **Chakras** Root

♡ **Care** Fades in direct sunlight

◊ **Water Cleansing** ☒ Y ☐ N

MAGIC Smoky Quartz is one of the most powerful crystal tools for energy transmutation (*transmutation = the action of changing, or the state of being changed into another form*). Smoky Quartz holds a similar cleansing magic as its cousin Amethyst, but where Amethyst goes high, Smoky Quartz goes deep: this dusky crystal moves energies out of your aura, swiftly carrying them deep into the earth for transmutation. Smoky Quartz makes a phenomenal meditation partner, as it is simultaneously stabilizing and consciousness-expanding. Follow your own intuition as you experiment with adding it to your meditation practice; I like to place a crystal at the base of my spine (between my inner thighs), and a crystal touching the sole of each foot. If you don't have a meditation practice, simply taking a nap with a Smoky Quartz in bed with you can work rejuvenating miracles. Or try a **Smoky Soak**, one of my favorite ways to relax and melt the day's stress away: place a Smoky Quartz crystal on each corner of your bathtub (if your tub doesn't have corners, simply put the crystals in the water with you). Add some Rose Quartz to your bathwater for an extra dose of self-care and *aaahhh*... instant relaxation and deep healing. Enjoy your time soaking in this sacred magic. Smoky Quartz is helpful anywhere and everywhere, so keep this energy powerhouse wherever you feel its smoky magic is needed.

NOTES Smoky Quartz's color is caused by natural exposure to gamma rays. Clear or lightly smoky crystals can be darkened with artificial gamma rays or heat exposure; very dark Smoky Quartz is usually treated.

AFFIRMATION
"I release whatever is ready to transform"

Sodalite

THE REAL YOU • TRUTH-TELLING • INTUITION

✴ **Color** Royal blue + white
◎ **Born in** Brazil, India, Canada
𓂀 **Chakras** Throat, 3rd Eye
◊ **Water Cleansing** ☒ Y ☐ N

MAGIC Sodalite is easily confused with Lapis Lazuli (and often sold as Lapis by less-than-honest dealers). Both are royal-blue crystals, and they both primarily resonate with the 3rd eye and throat chakras. They're definitely different, however; I think of Sodalite as the little sibling of Lapis Lazuli, as Sodalite is much less energetically intense. And sometimes less intense is exactly the right medicine for a situation — too much energy can be overwhelming and counterproductive for healing. *Less can be more.* If you're drawn to Sodalite, try meditating with it on your 3rd eye (*between your eyebrows*) to gently begin to get in touch with your inner world, the 'real you.' And if you're having a hard time getting clear on how you want to show up in the world, or bravely speaking your truth, spend some time with this gentle blue stone on your throat to help you begin to find your brave, true voice.

NOTES Named for its high sodium content, Sodalite almost always forms in non-crystallized masses, and is sold in a wide variety of polished shapes. Often confused with Lapis Lazuli (which is much rarer and more expensive), here are two things you can look for to tell them apart: 1) Sodalite usually shows more white coloring; 2) Sodalite does not have golden flecks of Pyrite, while Lapis often does, particularly high-grade Lapis. (*so-da-lite*)

AFFIRMATION
"I look within to find the real me"

Spinel

TRUST • INTUITION • EMPOWERMENT

⊛ **Color** Reds, pinks, blues +

⊘ **Born in** Sri Lanka, SE Asia, Tanzania

♋ **Chakras** Varies according to color

◇ **Water Cleansing** ☒ Y ☐ N

MAGIC Spinel is definitely a top contender for the 'Most Misunderstood + Under-Appreciated Gemstone' award. This multicolored gem has been mined and treasured since antiquity, but was usually mistaken for better-known gemstones, particularly Ruby and Sapphire. It was only in 1783 that the technology was developed to determine the difference, and — surprise! — it was discovered that many famous Rubies and Sapphires are actually Spinel, such as the giant centerpiece 'Ruby' in the Imperial State Crown (the gem-encrusted crown ritually worn by the British monarch for their most important events). Spinel continues to be under-appreciated today — let's change that! This beautiful gemstone deserves its own chance to shine, and get out of the shadow of its more-famous counterparts. Red-toned Spinel, the most common color, does hold many parallels to the magic of Ruby — strength, power, protection — but with a beautiful addition of *trust.* These are choose-your-own-adventure gemstones, 'Let-Go-And-Let-God' gemstones. Spinels of all colors will help you release into a deeper sense of trust: trust in the bigger picture, trust in divine timing, trust in yourself. What a precious, empowering gift.

NOTES Spinel crystallizes in a variety of colors, with brilliant reds the most common variety, also called **Ruby Spinel** *(pictured, in a white marble matrix).* Lab-grown Spinel can be created in all colors besides purple, and is commonly used in inexpensive jewelry. The most recent addition to the modern birthstone list (2016), Spinel is an August birthstone. *(spin-el)*

AFFIRMATION
"Trust is my superpower"

Spirit Quartz

JOY • GRATITUDE • GENEROSITY

✳ **Color** Lavender, clear, yellow

◎ **Born in** South Africa

♆ **Chakras** Crown, 3rd Eye, Heart

♡ **Care** Fades in direct sunlight

◊ **Water Cleansing** ☒ Y ☐ N

MAGIC *Crystallized Joy*. Sweet Spirit Quartz sends out sparkling vibrations of joy from each of its many crystal points, creating energy fireworks within the entire space surrounding it. A beautiful crystal of transcendence, Spirit Quartz helps you remember to radiate your magnificent energy *outward* into the world, purifying any tendencies toward self-absorption, and enhancing your ability to be compassionate, generous, and grateful. Spirit Quartz is my favorite crystal companion for making *gratitude lists*, my go-to practice for instantly transforming my energy to a higher vibration. I place one of these lavender crystals by my journal or computer as I free-write a list of things I feel grateful for in that moment, big and small.

This practice only takes a few minutes, and truly is a total vibration game changer — I can't recommend it enough! Spirit Quartz is very supportive for anyone whose work includes channeling healing and inspiration for others, and is an ideal crystal for healers, teachers, and creatives of all kinds. One of the most uplifting members of the crystal realm, this radiant crystal will spread inspiration, healing, and sparkles of joy wherever you keep it.

NOTES Spirit Quartz is a rare variety of Quartz, found only in one small area of South Africa. Most Spirit Quartz is a form of Amethyst; yellow specimens are sometimes called **Citrine Spirit Quartz**. **Cactus Quartz** is an alternate name, and single points covered with tiny crystals are sometimes called **Fairy Quartz**.

AFFIRMATION
"I am grateful for my magical life"

Stilbite

SPACE HOLDING • HEART OPENING • NURTURING

✳ **Color** Peach, white

🜚 **Born in** India

🝑 **Chakras** Crown, Heart

💧 **Water Cleansing** ☒ Y ☐ N

MAGIC Pearly Stilbite is a space-holding crystal. This gentle crystal doesn't 'move' energies, like so many crystals; instead, it creates a peaceful bubble of energy around people and places, holding space for everyone around it to simply Be. *You are enough.* Peach-colored Stilbite crystals also have a gentle heart-opening energy. Stilbite often forms in stunning clusters with other minerals, most commonly Apophyllite and Chalcedony. As Apophyllite is a powerful energy cleanser, Stilbite + Apophyllite clusters make spaces feel energetically fresh and nurturing. And Chalcedony is one of the most soothing crystals, so Stilbite + Chalcedony clusters create an ultra calming, zen-like atmosphere. Sweet Stilbite is helpful and nurturing in any room of the house, and is a perfect crystal for healing spaces.

NOTES Stilbite is in the zeolite family, a group of more than 40 water-containing silicate minerals (Scolecite and Tanzanite are other zeolites featured in this book). It is mined primarily for industrial use. Stilbite has a pearly luster, and crystallizes in a unique variety of shapes, including globular clusters, fan-shaped crystals, and 'bow-tie' formations. It commonly forms combined with other minerals such as Apophyllite *(pictured)*, Calcite, and Chalcedony. The mineral **Heulandite** is very close in appearance to Stilbite — they were considered to be the same mineral until 1818 — and has similar metaphysical energies. *(still-bite)*

AFFIRMATION
"I am enough"

Sugilite

INTUITIVE GUIDANCE • INNER KNOWING • CLARITY

⊛ **Color** Vibrant violet + purple
⌖ **Born in** South Africa
◇ **Chakras** 3rd Eye, Crown
◊ **Water Cleansing** ☒ Y ☐ N

MAGIC *Inner knowing.* Violet-colored Sugilite could be a magical talisman for you if you need help reconnecting with your intuition — that inner voice which has all the answers you're looking for. Like putting on a pair of new glasses, Sugilite can help clear away inner fog, so you can more easily attune to your inner knowing. When your mind is spinning in overwhelm, grab your Sugilite, find a quiet spot, and take a moment to simply stop. Stop overthinking, stop looping, stop mind-spinning. Just sit quietly, breathing calmly, and drop into that place where you feel your intuition — usually it's in your belly or heart. Ask: *"What would you like me to know right now, Inner Voice?"* Breathe, and feel into the answers. Your inner voice will always know what to do.

NOTES Discovered in Japan in 1944, today Sugilite primarily comes from one deposit in South Africa, and commonly forms blended with black manganese. Almost always opaque, a tiny percentage of Sugilite is transparent, called **Gel Sugilite**. A rarer mineral, Sugilite is mostly sold in small polished pieces, tumbled stones, and cabochons. Sometimes called **Lavulite / Luvulite**. Sugilite is commonly pronounced incorrectly; the [g] should sound like the word 'gut.' *(soo-guh-lite)*

AFFIRMATION
"I listen to my intuition"

Sulfur

POSITIVITY • CREATIVITY • IMMUNITY BOOST

⊛ **Color** Neon yellow

◷ **Born in** Bolivia, Italy

❀ **Chakras** Solar Plexus

♡ **Care** Fragile

◊ **Water Cleansing** ☐ Y ☒ N

MAGIC Ever wondered what the biblical phrase 'fire and brimstone' referred to? Well you're in luck, my friend, wonder no more: this neon crystal is real-life brimstone! Born from ancient volcanic activity, crystallized Sulfur is a fantastic helper for detoxifying, purifying, and uplifting. Do you get stuck in 'glass-half-empty' thinking? Bring a piece of this sunshine stone into your life and let it work its sunny magic to transform your mood and uplift your outlook. Holding a joyfully fizzy energy, Sulfur's neon vibes help remind you to live with a sense of childlike wonder. This is a fun crystal for spaces where you get creative, whether that's a corporate cubicle or artist atelier. Great for increasing immune system vitality and strength, Sulfur's energy feels like a happy giggle encapsulated in a crystal; hold it to your solar plexus when you need a bubbly boost of sunshine. And no, you're not imagining things: Sulfur crystals do have a faint — but unmistakable — eggy odor!

NOTES A pure element (S), Sulfur is mined worldwide for a variety of industrial uses, with crystallized specimens historically found near Italian volcanoes. Modern specimens mainly come from Bolivia, and often form in combination with a white mineral matrix. While Sulfur is not toxic, specimens may contain traces of minerals which are, so wash your hands after handling and keep away from little mouths. Sulfur crystals can crumble easily, and fade in prolonged sunlight. Also spelled Sulphur. (_suhl_-fur)

AFFIRMATION
"Happiness flows to me + through me"

Sunstone

CONFIDENCE • CREATIVITY • MANIFESTATION

✳ **Color** Glittering orange, red, brown

◎ **Born in** USA, India, Norway, Canada

⚘ **Chakras** Sacral, Solar Plexus

◌ **Water Cleansing** ☒ Y ☐ N

MAGIC I never felt a connection with Sunstone until I looked at one under bright sunlight, and wow; mesmerizing, technicolored sparkles suddenly leapt out from the depths of the stone. *It just needed a little light to show its magic*. And isn't that the same for all of us? We just need a little encouragement — a little sunlight! — to bring our sparkling inner gifts to life. Like a great coach or therapist, Sunstone helps you remember that you already have all the magic you need inside of you. This sacral + solar plexus crystal helps you connect with your inner creativity and confidence, and empowers you to let your inner light sparkle and shine. Don't hide in the shadows — *the world needs your magic now more than ever*. So let Sunstone help you bravely show up, shine bright, and share

your unique magic with the world. Sunstone = your crystal cheerleader, always cheering you on!

NOTES A member of the feldspar mineral family, Sunstone is filled with sparkling inclusions of Hematite and Goethite. **Oregon Sunstone**, a variety that is usually faceted into gemstones, contains Copper. High-end varieties such as **Rainbow Lattice Sunstone** (absolutely amazing — look it up!) can appear to contain strands of iridescent glitter. Sunstone is also called **Aventurine Feldspar**.

AFFIRMATION
"I am here to sparkle + shine"

Tangerine Quartz

SEXUAL HEALING • BODY ISSUES • FERTILITY

Color Shades of orange
Born in Brazil
Chakras Sacral
Water Cleansing ☒ Y ☐ N

MAGIC *Sexual Healing*. We all have things to heal related to sexuality and body image. Even if you're the unicorn among us who has had only 100% uplifting, body-affirming, consensual sexual experiences ***(anyone out there raising their hand?)***, stories of shame and transgressions run deep through each of our bloodlines and ancestral histories. Tangerine Quartz is a powerful crystal for liquidating and transforming stored shame, pain, and negative body associations and experiences. Place one of these dusky orange crystals on your low stomach or between your inner thighs, breathe deeply, and imagine a warm orange glow permeating your lower body, gently relaxing your hips, lower back, and sexual organs. If you feel the need for extra support, place grounding crystals like Smoky Quartz or Black Tourmaline touching the soles of your feet. Since Tangerine Quartz activates stagnant energy in your sacral chakra, this is also a fantastic crystal for lighting juicy fires in the bedroom. Put a small point under your mattress and thank me later.

NOTES Tangerine Quartz is the orange variation of Quartz + Hematite ***(to learn more about this crystal family, see page 158)***. As polishing would often remove the orange layer, these crystals usually have a matte finish and imperfect, chipped edges. Small crystal points are easiest to find; larger clusters are less common and can be expensive.

AFFIRMATION
"It is safe to be in my body"

Tanzanite

SOUL PURPOSE • VISION • INNER CLARITY

✳ **Color** Violet-blue

◎ **Born in** Tanzania

🪷 **Chakras** 3rd Eye, Throat, Crown

💧 **Water Cleansing** ☒ Y ☐ N

MAGIC *Honest clarity*. Born in the foothills of majestic Mount Kilimanjaro, Tanzanite clears away energy cobwebs from your 3rd eye, throat, and crown chakras, helping you get crystal-clear on the important questions of life: *"Who am I, why am I here, and what should I be doing with my one wild and precious life?"* It shares a similar energy with Iolite, another violet-blue crystal that also helps you get clear on your Inner Why, but a Tanzanite gemstone has the added beauty of being *dichroic*: its violet hues change color when viewed under different light sources. Wear this beautiful gemstone in jewelry to help you stay aligned with your soul's highest mission, and to keep true to your intuition. When you're confused which step to take next, ask your Tanzanite for help, and sit quietly with your crystal to let answers come into clarity.

NOTES One of the rarest gemstones, Tanzanite is a very 'young' crystal, discovered only in 1967 when a grassfire cleared a large area in the Kilimanjaro foothills. Because Tanzanite is brownish-red in its natural state it had gone unnoticed by locals, but after fire swept through the area the ground was decorated with bright blue stones, as Tanzanite turns blue when exposed to high heat (all Tanzanite gemstones are heat-treated). Affordable relative to its rarity, Tanzanite is in the zeolite mineral family, and was named by Tiffany & Co. in homage to Tanzania, the only known source. Tanzanite is a December birthstone. *(tan-zuh-nite)*

AFFIRMATION
"I am getting clear"

Tiger's Eye

COURAGE • EMPOWERMENT • PROTECTION

⊛ **Color** Iridescent golden-brown stripes
⌀ **Born in** South Africa, Australia, India
♧ **Chakras** Sacral, Solar Plexus, Root
♡ **Care** May be too intense for bedrooms
◊ **Water Cleansing** ☒ Y ☐ N

MAGIC I've polled my crystal-loving pals, and we all agree: Tiger's Eye brings to mind shag carpets and groovy looks. This shimmery stone really rocks those '70s vibes, and not only because it was a popular gemstone of the era. Tiger's Eye holds a strongly 'activating' energy, similar to the spirit of that volatile decade of intense social change. It's the energy of challenging the status quo, not being afraid to speak up, and breaking things to transform them for the better. If you are a social activist or crusader for change, this could be an important gemstone ally for you. Keep one close when you need to channel fierceness, or meditate with it placed on the chakra you would like to empower. Tiger's Eye also has a long history as a powerful protection talisman.

Although a classic favorite of little kids and men, I have found that this crystal can feel off-putting to some women. If you feel turned off by its vibration but wish to work with its energy, try seeking out a non-polished piece, as the energies of raw Tiger's Eye flow differently (I also recommend using Tiger's Eye in combination with an energy-moving crystal such as Amethyst, to help transmute any sticky energetic 'sludge' this crystal might loosen up). Or try **Tiger Iron** (also called **Mugglestone**), which combines layers of Tiger's Eye, Hematite, and Red Jasper into a deeply recharging, grounding crystal.

NOTES Tiger's Eye is a variety of Quartz filled with fibers that create luminescent bands, similar to the iridescence in a feline eye. Forming in several colors, golden-brown Tiger's Eye is by far the most common variety, followed by blue (also called **Hawk's Eye**). The red variety is almost always created with heat treatment.

AFFIRMATION
"I am fierce + fearless"

Topaz

NOBILITY • HIGHER SELF • HIGH VIBRATION

✳ **Color** Various
◉ **Born in** Brazil, Russia, Australia, Mexico
❀ **Chakras** Varies according to color
♡ **Care** Can fade in prolonged sunlight
◊ **Water Cleansing** ☒ Y ☐ N

MAGIC *Be Noble.* Topaz is an ancient gemstone that vibrates with 'noble' energy. Noble = Having high moral principles and ideals, aka being the type of person who chooses to do the right thing and walk the higher path whenever possible. *Turn the other cheek / Treat others the way you wish to be treated / Be the change you wish to see in the world = Noble.* Each color of this gemstone has its own particular resonance. Blue / Green Topaz helps you use your *words* nobly, so that you communicate with the highest vibration possible. Golden / Yellow / Orange / Brown Topaz helps you use your *actions* nobly, so that you create, share, and engage from a place of generosity and illumination. Pink Topaz helps you *love* nobly, so that you share your heart with deep

respect for everyone involved. And Clear Topaz helps your use your *presence* nobly, so that you walk through life with brilliance, grace, kindness, and luminance. Topaz = helping you remember to always choose the noble path, and vibrate at the highest level.

NOTES Topaz crystallizes in long, lozenge-like crystals, and occurs in a wide variety of colors. Prized for the ability to grow unusually large crystals of gem quality, Topaz gemstones are usually heat-treated to enhance and stabilize their color, as natural Topaz fades in sunlight. **Imperial Topaz** is a name used for several colors of high-quality specimens. **Mystic Topaz** is artificially coated with an iridescent layer (similar to an aura crystal). Golden Topaz is a November birthstone, and Blue Topaz is a December birthstone. *(tow-paz)*

AFFIRMATION
"I choose the highest vibration"

Black Tourmaline

PROTECTION · GROUNDING · BOUNDARIES

✳ **Color** Opaque jet-black
◉ **Born in** Brazil, China
♋ **Chakras** Root
◊ **Water Cleansing** ☒ Y ☐ N

MAGIC *The Crystal Bodyguard.* An energy heavyweight full of protective magic, Black Tourmaline is a must-have crystal for its skill at keeping you safely grounded in this physical reality. These black gems are vitally important for balancing the heady vibes generated by other crystals — keep one close for continuous grounding and recharging, and sleep with a crystal at your feet whenever you feel untethered or unsafe. As an energy protector Black Tourmaline is unparalleled; think of this crystal as a guard dog who tirelessly protects your boundaries and deflects negative energies. Place one near the entrance to your physical spaces (home, office, dorm room, etc) and it will tirelessly stand guard, keeping all dark forces out. Tuck a small piece into your clothing, pocket, or wallet for on-the-go protection, and definitely don't forget to stash one in your car to keep you safe on the road. With an ancient history of being used by magicians as a protective psychic shield, Black Tourmaline should be one of the first crystals you add to your collection, as it will keep you grounded and balanced as you continue down your path of sparkling, crystalline adventures.

NOTES Also known as **Schorl**, iron-rich Black Tourmaline is the most common Tourmaline variety, and by far the least expensive. Sometimes flecked with bits of silvery mica, Black Tourmaline is commonly available as both raw and polished specimens. Tourmaline is an October birthstone. *(tur-muh-leen)*

AFFIRMATION
"I am protected"

Colored Tourmaline

JOY • INNER CHILD • HEART HEALING

✳ **Color** Green, pink +

◎ **Born in** Brazil, Africa

◇ **Chakras** Heart

◊ **Water Cleansing** ☒ Y ☐ N

MAGIC Colored Tourmalines are such joyful crystals! These gemstones hold an irresistible magic for people who feel a strong connection with their inner child, as they encourage a childlike sense of open-hearted curiosity, playfulness, and unconditional love. If you ever feel like you're stuck in a rut of taking life (or yourself) a little too seriously, spend some time with a colorful Tourmaline to (en)lighten up! Green and pink are the most common colors, and as our heart chakras resonate to both colors these crystals are powerful heart-healers, especially when it comes to heartbreak related to sadness and trauma originating in childhood. Tourmalines that are multicolored (**Watermelon** or **Bi-Color Tourmaline**) are extra special, as they help balance the dance of Yin (feminine) + Yang (masculine) energies within you. They also combine both heart chakra colors into one very beautiful gemstone. Let Tourmaline flow its healing magic into all the parts of you that need some extra joy, love, and beauty.

NOTES Most colored Tourmaline gemstones are varieties of **Elbaite Tourmaline**, found worldwide in a variety of colors. They crystallize in long, prismatic crystals. Their varietal names are **Rubellite** (pink / red), **Verdelite** (green) and **Indicolite** (blue-green). **Paraiba Tourmaline** is a sales name used for high-quality Tourmaline; the name was originally used for top-grade Tourmaline from the Brazilian state of Paraiba, as magnificent specimens were found there starting in the late 1980s, but it is now also used for specimens from other locations. Tourmaline is an October birthstone. (*tur-muh-lin*)

AFFIRMATION
"I choose joy"

Tourmaline Quartz

BALANCE • TRAUMA HEALING • BOUNDARIES

✳ **Color** Translucent white + black

◉ **Born in** Brazil

✿ **Chakras** Crown, Root

◊ **Water Cleansing** ☒ Y ☐ N

MAGIC *You grow through what you go through.* Tourmaline Quartz blends together two powerful crystals from opposite ends of the energy spectrum: Black Tourmaline, energy bodyguard extraordinaire and one of the best grounding crystals, and Clear Quartz, master energy purifier and vibration transmitter. This duality makes Tourmaline Quartz a supercharged crystal of balance, growth, and emotional support. This is a wonderful support stone to work with when you feel 'triggered,' aka when something traumatic from your past is activated in the present moment. Being triggered often makes someone feel one of two ways: blazingly angry, or numbly frozen. When you feel this happening, take your Tourmaline Quartz and find a quiet, safe space. Tune into your body: where in your body are you feeling triggered? Hold your crystal to that spot, and *breathe*. In and out, in and out. Allow Tourmaline Quartz to work its supportive magic and create a safe space all around you. You are here. You are safe. *You are healing.*

NOTES Tourmaline Quartz (also called **Tourmalinated Quartz**) is translucent to transparent Quartz filled with clumps or 'needles' of Black Tourmaline. It is most commonly sold as polished specimens and tumbled stones, and is primarily found in Brazil. *(tur-muh-lin)*

AFFIRMATION
"It is safe for me to heal"

Turquoise

EARTH WISDOM • NATURE MAGIC • PROTECTION

⊛ **Color** Opaque blue + green
⊘ **Born in** USA, China, Iran
☗ **Chakras** Throat, 3rd Eye
⬙ **Water Cleansing** ☐ Y ☒ N

MAGIC *Stone of Earth and Sky.* Bright Turquoise has an ancient history as a revered gemstone, long beloved by indigenous cultures, royalty, and hippie glam alike. A classic adornment on boho fingers and wrists the world over, Turquoise's history as sacred jewelry stretches far back through the mists of time, as it was one of the first gemstones to be mined. Native Americans revere blue-green Turquoise as a sacred representation of the bridge between heaven and earth: Blue Turquoise = Father Sky, Green Turquoise = Mother Earth. Wear Turquoise to strengthen your commitment to walking lightly on the planet, and living in awareness and reverence of natural cycles. A stone of folklore wisdom and nature magic, Turquoise magnifies your connection to the wisdom in your own indigenous histories, however many generations back in your lineage your indigenous ancestors lived. Worn as a protective talisman by everyone from ancient Aztecs and Egyptians, to modern Tibetans and Native Americans, Turquoise can also form a protective armor around you, shielding and strengthening you as you walk forward in Integrity and Truth.

NOTES Turquoise forms in non-crystallized masses. Most Turquoise used in jewelry has been *stabilized*, a chemical process that hardens porous specimens to make them suitable for jewelry. Imitation Turquoise is extremely common, especially blue-dyed Howlite (sometimes sold as **Howlite Turquoise** or **Turquenite**). **White Turquoise** and **White Buffalo Turquoise** are Howlite. **African Turquoise** is a variety of Jasper. Turquoise is a December birthstone. *(tur-kwoiz)*

AFFIRMATION
"I am one with nature."

Unakite

HEART HEALING • EMPATH SUPPORT • NURTURING

✳ **Color** Opaque green + red

⦿ **Born in** USA, South Africa

⚘ **Chakras** Heart

◊ **Water Cleansing** ☒ Y ☐ N

MAGIC Formed from a combination of green Epidote and red Feldspar, Unakite blends both heart chakra colors together into this gentle heart-tonic crystal. Unakite is a support stone for empaths, so if you feel like your heart breaks a million times a day from the world's stories and sadnesses, Unakite would be a very supportive tool to help you avoid empath overwhelm. My favorite way to connect with Unakite's healing vibration is this bathtime ritual:

RITUAL Fill your tub with warm water, your favorite bubbles, and a few drops of an earthy essential oil like eucalyptus, pine, cedar, or frankincense. Get in, and place a Rose Quartz and black or gray crystal by your feet, to ground yourself in a loving self-care vibration. Gently place a Unakite crystal on your chest. Close your eyes, and imagine that the Unakite is a soft piece of green moss, covering your heart like a protective blanket. Breathe in the scent of the essential oils, and relax into the warm water cradling your entire body. Know that you are very safe, and very protected. Allow yourself to nurture and renew your tender heart with tears, if they need to flow. *Your tender heart is nurtured and protected.*

NOTES Unakite is technically a 'rock,' as it is a combination of several minerals: Epidote, Feldspar, and occasionally Quartz. It occurs only in *massive* (non-crystallized) form, and is mostly sold as small tumbled stones and polished pieces. Unakite is named after the Unaka mountain range that borders North Carolina and Tennessee (USA), where it was first identified in 1874. Also called **Unakite Jasper**. *(you-nuh-kite)*

AFFIRMATION
"My tender heart is nurtured + protected"

Vanadinite

BOUNDARIES • DISCIPLINE • FOCUS

✴ **Color** Fiery red + orange

◎ **Born in** Morocco, USA, Mexico

🪷 **Chakras** Root, Sacral, Solar Plexus

💧 **Water Cleansing** ☐ Y ☒ N

MAGIC *Check yourself before you wreck yourself.* Vanadinite crystals are glossy-red hexagons that give you direction... remind you of anything? Okay, I hear you; stop signs are octagonal, not hexagonal like these crystals. But hear me out, friend: the magic of stop signs lies not in their shape, but in their ability to give direction and structure. And Vanadinite, with its striking resemblance, holds a similar power. Let me explain: we each have only so many hours a day in which we can do deeply focused and productive work, right? So how do you make sure you're using your limited time and energy to move forward on your biggest dreams and goals, aka the true work you're here to do? By having the discipline to *stay in your own lane*. And that's where Vanadinite comes in. It will keep you in your own lane, so you stay focused on your own work and magic. Vanadinite helps you maintain strong boundaries, structure, and focus — both in your personal and work lives. So keep this vibrant crystal in spaces where you Get To Work — your office, your writing nook, your workshop, your atelier. Let Vanadinite support you as you navigate the twists and turns of life, and help you stay on the path towards your truest, biggest purpose.

NOTES First identified in the 1800s, Vanadinite's discoverers were so taken by its unique appearance that they named it after the Norse goddess of beauty, *Vanadis*. Mined mainly for industrial use, Vanadinite forms as small hexagonal crystals, often on a rock matrix. It is also common as a coating on barite crystals. Vanadinite is lead-based, so keep out of reach of little mouths. *(vuh-nah-dih-nite)*

AFFIRMATION

"I am manifesting my authentic magic"

Vera Cruz Amethyst

WISH-MAKING • MIRACLES • JOY

✳ **Color** Translucent lavender

◎ **Born in** Mexico

🪷 **Chakras** Crown, 3rd Eye, Heart

💧 **Water Cleansing** ☒ Y ☐ N

MAGIC Found in only one spot on our planet — the mossy mountains of Veracruz, Mexico — Vera Cruz Amethyst is beloved for its breathtaking glow and miracle-making vibration. These lavender crystals are manifestation tools that can help bring your biggest wishes to life, as they contain the transformative powers of Amethyst upleveled with an extra sprinkling of dreams-come-true magic.

RITUAL Hold a Vera Cruz up to your 3rd eye (*between your eyebrows*) and imagine the outcome or feeling you are wishing for. Take your time, breathe, don't rush through this — you are infusing the crystal with your wish. Next, hold the crystal to your lips and blow on it, like you're blowing out the candles on a birthday cake. Place your wish-infused crystal somewhere you will see it regularly. Every time you see your luminescent Vera Cruz, let it be a reminder that you live in a universe humming with limitless miracles and magical moments. Have endless faith and expect unlimited grace, because God / Goddess / Source Energy / The Universe *(whichever your preferred word for divinity)* always has your back — all the time, everywhere, and in every way.

NOTES Vera Cruz Amethyst's delicate lavender color and exceptional translucency set it apart from other Amethyst varieties. A rarer form of Amethyst, it forms in thin, elongated crystals, and is most commonly sold as individual crystal points. Amethyst is a February birthstone. *(ver-uh-crooz)*

AFFIRMATION
"I expect miracles"

Zircon

PERSPECTIVE • GRATITUDE • GROUNDING

✳ **Color** Golden-brown, blue, clear +

◎ **Born in** Australia, South Africa

♨ **Chakras** Varies according to color

♡ **Care** Can fade in prolonged sunlight

◊ **Water Cleansing** ☒ Y ☐ N

MAGIC Zircon is another top contender for the 'Most Misunderstood + Under-Appreciated Gemstone' award, mostly because it's often confused with Cubic Zirconia (CZ), an inexpensive synthetic crystal. Zircon is a natural and ancient gemstone — actually, it's *the* most ancient mineral we've found on earth, with some crystals carbon-dated to over four billion years ago, long before humans were a twinkle in the universe's eye. I find it absolutely breathtaking that we can adorn ourselves with something so ancient and primordial, don't you? And yes, I say adorn because you're most likely to encounter this special gemstone in jewelry. This ancient crystal is a powerful talisman for grounding yourself in the truth of your place in the universe. Let it be a reminder that you are connected to the beginning of time itself through the minerals which make up your body — you are literally made of stardust. So don't be afraid to live your life to the fullest, magic maker. You can't 'mess this up.' You can't 'do life wrong.' You are a part of an incredible legacy that has been in the making since time began. That you are right here, right now, is an absolute miracle. *You are a living miracle*. So embrace the miracle that you are, magic maker, and live: live boldly, truthfully, bravely, magically... **LIVE!!!**

NOTES Usually originating as golden-brown crystals, Zircon is one of the only colored gemstones to show *brilliance* when faceted (internal rainbow sparkles, similar to Diamonds). Blue and clear gemstones — the most popular colors — are almost always created with heat-treatment. Blue Zircon is a December birthstone. *(zur-con)*

AFFIRMATION
"My life is a miracle"

#Goals

One last thing...

The 'goal' of working with crystals isn't to magically conjure up a 'perfect' life for yourself; the perfect romance, body, career, bank account, etc etc etc...

These are all wonderful things to have, of course, but focusing on them means missing out on the source of true happiness, and the point of this whole 'being a human' experience. Instead, the greatest magic to be gained from working with crystals (and from all forms of 'self-help,' truly) is that it supports you in becoming the clearest, shiniest, most inspired, and authentic version of yourself. So that you have a deep reservoir of wellbeing from which to share your unique kindness, care, and love with everyone your life touches. **Less self-help, more everyone-help.**

Because that, dear crystal friend, is what it's really all about. Radiate kindness, compassion, and love, and I promise that the 'perfect' life you desire will be all yours.

ABOUT THE AUTHOR

Guided by a mission to bring holistic wellness and vibrational healing into the mainstream, Yulia Van Doren is the founder of the trendsetting crystal brand, **Goldirocks**, and a Grammy-nominated international opera singer and sound healer. She has had the honor of training with leading teachers in consciousness, healing, and sound from an early age, and has trained in gemology at the Gemological Institute of America.

Her crystal books pioneered a new concept in crystal healing, with their combination of a relatable modern voice and beautiful design. Beloved worldwide, *The Modern Guide To Crystal Healing* series has won awards, been translated into multiple languages, and is the top-selling crystal series published in the last decade.

Yulia shares workshops, performances, and private healing sessions worldwide, and currently lives in the golden foothills of Northern California. She unequivocally believes that magic is 100% real, and available to everyone.

www.goldirocks.co
www.yuliavandoren.com

Thank You:

Mother Earth for the holy, healing gifts that are crystals.

My teachers, healers, and guides: I am grateful beyond what words
can express.

The Quadrille team for your vision, creativity, and support, especially Harriet
(you changed my life!).

The creatives whose magic graces every page of this book, especially
Angela, Erika, Vanessa, Gemma, and Ingrid.

Those who shared their beautiful crystals, spaces, and objects, especially
Kitkitdizzi, The Sunroom, Christiansen Mineral Connection,
Bebe Winch, Paradigm Jewelry, and The Fossil Cartel.

Everyone who has supported Goldirocks and my previous books: Thank you for
supporting this sparkling adventure so wholeheartedly. And that includes **you**,
magic maker — your healing makes this world a more radiant place for
us all. I can't wait to see the magic you create!

My Beloveds: You know who you are. Thank you for filling my life with
your magic and love. None of this would exist without you.
I love you with all my heart.

Photography credits:

Managing Director Sarah Lavelle

Senior Commissioning Editor Harriet Butt

Assistant Editor Oreolu Grillo

Series Designer Vanessa Masci

Designers Claire Rochford and
Gemma Hayden

Cover Design Yulia Van Doren

Photographers Angela Nunnink,
Erika Raxworthy, and Yulia Van Doren

Props Stylists Yulia Van Doren and
Priscilla Moscatt

Picture Reseacher Chinh Hoang

Production Director Stephen Lang

Production Controller Katie Jarvis

Published in 2023 by Quadrille,
an imprint of Hardie Grant Publishing

Quadrille

52—54 Southwark Street

London SE1 1UN

quadrille.com

text © Yulia Van Doren 2023

design © Quadrille 2023

ISBN 978 183 783 079 4

Printed with soy inks in China

*No medical claims are made for the stones in this
book and the information given is not intended
to act as a substitute for medical treatment. The
healing properties are given for guidance only
and are, for the most part, based on anecdotal
evidence and/or traditional therapeutic use.
The advice in this book is intended solely for
informational and educational purposes and
not as medical advice. If in any doubt, a crystal
healing practitioner or medical professional should
be consulted.*

David and Fela Shapell

dedicate this book
in memory of
their parents and relatives
who perished in the Holocaust.